LANGUAGE
OF FAITH

LANGUAGE
OF FAITH

A Selection from the

Most Expressive Jewish Prayers

Original Text & New English Verse Translations

Gathered and Edited by

NAHUM N. GLATZER

SCHOCKEN BOOKS   NEW YORK

[◩]

The illustration on the cover is reproduced from a Festival Prayer Book handwritten on vellum, 1380, probably in the Rhineland. Gates of Mercy, prayer for the Day of Atonement. Louis M. Rabinowitz Collection, The New York Public Library.

Library of Congress Cataloging-in-Publication Data
Language of faith.
English and Hebrew.
1. Judaism—Prayer-books and devotions—English.
2. Judaism—Prayer-books and devotions—Hebrew.
I. Glatzer, Nahum Norbert, 1903–
BM665.G58   1988   296.7'2   88-18377
ISBN 0-8052-0911-5

TO THE MEMORY OF SALMAN SCHOCKEN

1877‑1959

CONTENTS

Preface   13

Introduction   17

CREATION

You Are He Who Was   40

A Hymn on Creation   42

May the Name Send His Hidden Light   44

Who at His Word Makes Evening Fall   46

Creator of Light   48

Shaper of Origins   50

Meditation Before the "Sanctification"   52

Meditation on the Creation of Man   54

Blessing of the New Moon   56

A Perfect World   58

THE PRESENCE OF GOD

My Soul Thirsteth for Thee   62

From Eternity to Eternity   64

Whosoever Knoweth Thy Name   66

With All My Strength   68

Lord, Where Shall I Find Thee?   70

Lord of the Universe . . . If You Had Cattle   72

Heart's Companion   74

Whom Have I in Heaven but Thee?   76

The Song of "You"   80

And Yet I Pray   82

MY TIMES ARE IN THY HAND

I Trust in Thee   86
Man's Way Is Not His Own   88
What Is Man?   90
O Lord, Thou Lover of Souls   92
I Was Resolved to Do His Will   94
God, God of the Spirits   96
Thou and I   98
Enable Us to Break Desire   100
Humility   102
Father of All Worldly Things   104
Forgive Me   106

DE PROFUNDIS

From the Depths I Called Thee   110
The Lord Is My Shepherd   112
I Sat Alone Because of Thy Hand   114
In My Straits I Called   116
Thou Hast Helped Me to Salvation   120
The World Lies in Darkness   122
Hear Our Voice   124
The Gates of Mercy   126
The God of Them That Repent   128
Let Me Return   130
Give Me a Good Heart   132
Do Your Will   134

THANKSGIVING

The Soul You Have Placed in Me   138
Grace after Meals   140
Creator of Many Souls   142
After Deliverance from Danger   144
My Father Art Thou   146
Wise in Thy Truth   148
Streams in Dry Ground   150
Well I Know   152
Father of Life   154
Blessing of Death   156

KNOWLEDGE

With Thee Is Wisdom   160
The Gift of Knowledge   162
Our Father, the Father Compassionate   164
Thou Hast Taught Us Knowledge   166
That Thy Torah Be Our Craft   168
The Crown of Torah   170

THE CYCLE OF LIFE

The Blessing after the Circumcision   174
Bridegroom and Bride   176
Grant Them Mercy   178
Into Thine Hand   180
Who Drops the Bonds of Sleep   182

Bless Thou . . . This Year   184

Thou Givest All, Taking Nought   186

Who Formed You in Judgment   190

Kaddish   192

Memorial Prayer   194

ISRAEL: SUFFERING SERVANT

Watchman of Israel   198

Our Eyes Are Longing   200

Our Brothers, All the House of Israel   202

Thou Hast Made Me Hunger   204

Against the Will of Heaven   206

The Martyr's Prayer   208

A Marrano's Prayer upon Awakening   210

A Marrano's Morning Prayer   212

A Bar Mitzvah Prayer   214

Passover, Bergen-Belsen, 1944   216

Lord, I Want to Return   218

Rock of Israel   222

ZION

When a Foreigner   226

Leave Us Not   228

Thy City and Thy People   230

Jerusalem, Thou Holy City   232

Take Pity, O Lord   234

Comfort, O Lord   236

From a Judaeo-Greek Lament   240

The Sanctity of Zion   242

O God, Save Masada   244

Before the Battle   246

The Return   248

SABBATH

Accept Our Rest   252

Blessed Be the Name   254

Lord of All Eons   258

A Meditation before the Conclusion of the Sabbath   260

Who Sets Apart the Sacred and Profane   262

God of Abraham   264

DAYS OF AWE

Grant Thy Awe   270

It Is for Us to Praise   272

Therefore We Hope for Thee   274

Reign over All the Universe   276

Remembrance   278

Before I Was Formed   280

Our God Who Art in Heaven   282

I Shall Flee from Thee to Thee   284

The Reader's Prayer   286

Thou Givest a Hand to Transgressors   290

The Dwellers on High   292

Illumine My Eyes   294

Open unto Us the Gate   296

The Closing of the Gate   298

PEACE

Set Peace, Goodness and Blessing   302

Walk Me in Peace   304

Love and Brotherliness   306

Keep My Tongue from Evil   308

No Hatred   310

Lord of Peace   312

Annul Wars and the Shedding of Blood   314

Guard Us from Vicious Leanings   316

May He Bless Thee   318

Notes and Acknowledgments   321

Guide to the Prayers   333

PREFACE

In the year 1947, Schocken Books initiated its Library series
with the publication of *Language of Faith - Selected Jewish Prayers.*
The publisher considered this volume "a declaration of inten-
tions" of the entire series, which was to cultivate the "great
classical traditions of Judaism." *Language of Faith* has long been
out of print. The generous reception accorded to this book
encouraged the plan of an expanded selection from the literature of prayers, hymns, liturgic poetry, and private devotions.

More than any other type of literature, prayer expresses the
deepest concerns of a person or a community of faith. Therefore, an attempt has been made to present examples from as
many historic periods and religious backgrounds as possible.
The selections include biblical passages; prayers from six apocryphal writings and from the newly discovered writings of the
Dead Sea sectarian community; devotions of the talmudic masters; some ancient Jewish prayers preserved by early Christian
literature; hymns of Jewish mystics from Germany, Spain, and
the Land of Israel, ancient and modern; liturgic poetry by
thinkers, moralists, and poets from the medieval and early
modern periods, including one of the prayers found in the
Cairo Genizah; hasidic prayers, especially those attributed to
Nahman of Bratzlav; samples of a Karaite and a Yemenite
prayer; *Tehinnot,* or private devotions of womenfolk; and, naturally, prayers of various origins that were made a part of the

daily and festival prayer book of both the Ashkenazic and the Sephardic rite. Modern prayer poetry, Western, Hebrew, and Israeli, is represented as well.

The literary forms vary from the most humble utterance to the more elaborate creation of the artist: from the grandeur of the Psalms and Judah Halevi's hymns to the naïveté of the medieval herdsman or the crude Bar Mitzvah prayer of the boy in a camp for displaced persons. In all of them we discern the basic simplicity of faith, and the pathos of a person aware of the presence of God. Voices, different in tone, mood, and strength, are united into one chorus, addressing the eternal "thou."

In becoming the central act performed thrice daily in the home or in the Synagogue, prayer was exposed to the danger of losing that spontaneity without which it is mere formula. Yet prayer has had sufficient inner strength to withstand convention. It has remained a living language and an expression of faith.

Prayer is a growing organism; this is symbolically indicated by the fact that this edition includes pieces which were either unknown or nonexistent when the first edition was being prepared: the hymns of the Dead Sea community in the past, and the prayers emanating from the experiences of the Jewish catastrophe in Europe and the building and defense of Israel in our own generation. It is the chief care of this selection to point to these aspects of Jewish prayer and liturgy.

With a few exceptions, the original texts, occasionally abbreviated (and, in the case of the Apocrypha, re-translated into Hebrew), face the renditions in English. Most of the texts are, of course, in Hebrew. The reader who knows Hebrew will wish to refer to the original and, on occasion, may wish to use it. Yet even those who cannot read the original will enjoy the simple apprehension of its form. The translations used (but occasionally altered) are listed in the Notes; thanks are due to the publishers and authors who have graciously given permis⁄ sion to use their material.

Where no translator is mentioned, the rendition was made by the editor, in cooperation with T. Herzl Rome. Alas, while preparing the manuscript for publication, Mr. Rome passed suddenly away (August 21, 1965). The volume owes much to his exquisite literary and artistic sense, youthful enthusiasm, and personal concern.

The selections retained from the first edition of *Language of Faith* appear in the translations by Olga Marx and Jacob Sloan, respectively, revised in places. As a rule, God is ad⁄ dressed as "thou"; however, in certain selections, especially those from popular devotional writings, "you" is used. The Notes give the most essential bibliographical and historical information.

The book is dedicated to the memory of Salman Schocken, among whose many achievements not the least remarkable was his deep understanding of, and love for, medieval Hebrew poetry, its form and its faith.

N. N. GLATZER

Brandeis University
Waltham, Mass.
December 14, 1966

"My heart is Thy place and Thou art my place."   SOLOMON IBN GABIROL

"The perfect good that can come to man is to cleave to Him, and this achievement is the secret of genuine prayer."   HASDAI CRESCAS

"Forget everybody and everything during your prayer; forget yourself and your needs. Then in truth you may worship God." NAHMAN OF BRATZLAV

"The sum and substance of the whole of historical Judaism, its handbook and memorial tablet, will ever be the prayer book."   FRANZ ROSENZWEIG

INTRODUCTION

What is Prayer?

The history of prayer and the attitude to prayer reflect the development and intellectual growth of humanity as a whole. Prayer appears in the most primitive societies, where it is related to charms and spells, magic attempts to force the deity or the spirit into human service, intertwined with endeavors to gain control over hostile powers or, at least, to mitigate their threat to man. Primitive man prays for assistance in the pursuit of egoistic aims; he petitions for things material; he utters paradoxical wishes. The Ewe tribesman prays: "Mawu Sogble!" ("Grant that brandy does not make me drunk.") He insists that his will be done. A Zulu to the ancestral ghost: "Help me or you will feed on nettles."

At the other end of the spectrum is the mystic's prayer. Here the soul, utterly free from material desires and expectations, rises to the divine, and concentrates on the source of all being; it is lonely with the Lonely (in the words of Plotinus). In this state prayer may lose its ability to make full use of the medium of language and fall into a monotonous recitation of praise, or into silence in the immediate presence of God.

Between the two extremes of the primitive and the mystical attitudes to prayer stretches the wide and variegated field of classical worship. Its common denominator is established by a religious consciousness that has emancipated itself from the mythical interrelationship of all things and from the notion of the interdependence of man, universe, and the gods. It is a religious consciousness that has come to realize the abyss between man, the finite creature; world, the realm of objects; and God, the transcendental being. In the introductory lecture in his *Major Trends in Jewish Mysticism,* G. G. Scholem has pointed out that at this stage of religious consciousness it is only the voice which can bridge the gulf between the human being and the divine: "the voice of God, directing and law-giving in His revelation, and the voice of man in prayer."

Thus it is man's response to the divine voice and his own voice raised in prayer that admit him into communion with the divine. Prayer, therefore, is at the very base of the mono-theist religions and precedes definite creeds and formulations of beliefs. "Prayer is religion in act," says William James. "It is prayer that distinguishes the religious phenomenon from such similar or neighboring phenomena as purely moral or aesthetic sentiment. Religion is . . . the vital act by which the entire mind seeks to save itself by clinging to the principle from which

it draws its life. This act is prayer, by which term I understand . . . the very movement itself of the soul, putting itself in
a personal relation of contact with the mysterious power of
which it feels the presence" (*The Varieties of Religious Experience,* Lecture XIX).

The term "personal relation," used by James, calls for emphasis. It is indeed a fundamental premise of prayer that the
speaker is as aware of the personal element in the One Whom
he addresses as he is conscious of his own self. Fully cognizant
of his insignificance within the totality of things, his dependence
on natural laws, he, nevertheless, senses in himself that component of the personal that permits him, even compels him,
to address himself to God, who despite His majesty and incom-
prehensibility evokes in man a faith in his ability to address
Him as Thou. In prayer man finds himself in a dialogical
relationship, which the medieval poet Judah Halevi defined
thus:

Going out to meet thee
I found thee coming toward me.

In this sphere of the personal relation, all human aspirations,
all that man wishes to achieve (including that for which he
must exert his own effort) turn into petition. Seneca erred
when he said it is "foolish to pray for a good spirit since you
can win that of yourself." Prayer in the classical sense does
not imply passivity on the part of man. It does not replace but
heightens and ennobles human enterprise. Man engages in
moral perfection, in attainment of knowledge, in social action,

but considers the fruits of his labor as free gifts, as answers to his prayers. The Platonic Socrates prayed for what he considered the aim of man's own strivings: "Beloved Pan . . . give me beauty of the inward soul, and may the outward and the inward man be at one" (*Phaedrus*, end).

The basic structure of prayer, therefore, consists of these three elements: the I of the human person, the thou of God who is addressed, and that which motivates man's turning to God: adoration, confession, outcry, thanksgiving, petition (be it for sustenance, for strength, for knowledge, for love, or for salvation). "My God, I trust in thee," words scratched on the walls of a Gestapo prison cell, "Bless thou this year," from the Jewish Prayer of Benedictions, and the talmudic "Whatever is good in your eyes, do"—invocations so different in content and implication are united by the fact that it is a person who speaks and God who is spoken to.

Unlike Diderot, who exclaimed, "O God, I ask nothing from thee, for if thou art not, the course of nature is an inner necessity, and if thou art, it is thy command," the devout person will pray not merely because "God exists," but because he senses the personal element that relates him to the divine and that calls for an expression in human language.

In this sphere of the personal, too, originates, on the highest rung, the religious experience of love, voiced in the prayers with so much freedom and abandon. It is this love that silences supplications for transitory goods; at least, it merges the quests of the individual with the needs and wants of the community, or of suffering mankind at large. In essence, such prayer will be pure hymn and song of adoration, an expression of the worshipper's consciousness of his task as thanksgiver for, and laudator of, the created world. In contradistinction to Ivan Karamazov's "I accept God, but I do not accept his world," the speaker is eternally grateful for the world, because, as comprehended by him, it comes from the Lord. If he prays "for" something, it is for the divine presence in human life and for the ability to pray. "O Lord, open thou my lips, and my mouth shall declare thy praise" (Psalm 51:17). God may at times be considered as "hiding His face" from man and world; man may at times feel himself to be utterly undeserving of response; but once the element of the personal is discovered and affirmed, there is trust in the possibility of "return," in the eventual restoration of the bond between God and man. Many of the Hebrew prayers, both biblical and post-biblical, are but supplications for this re-establishment of "the personal relation of contact," the renewal of life under the covenant.

Job is terrified by God's silence. More than by his own suffering, more than by the knowledge of the injustice of the world's government, he is plagued by the fear that his outcry, "Oh that I had one to hear me; lo, here is my signature, let the Almighty answer me" (31:35), will die unheeded. When, finally, "the Lord answered Job" (38:1), He made no loving reference to Job's personal predicament, nor did He offer a solution of the world's enigma; the sufferer's trust was restored by the very fact of the divine confrontation, for through it the neutral power acting in nature turned again into a thou, open to the human word and responding to it. Only when man has lost faith in the possibility of such response is he compelled to withhold his own word and let a vast realm of silence grow between his soul within and the world without. Jean Paul has depicted the solitude of the man without faith to whom the universe appears as "the cold, iron mask of a formless eternity." His anguished question, "Father, where are you?" cannot be answered. "There is no God" (*Siebenkaes,* second volume, end). No one expressed this solitude better than Nietzsche: "That world is well hidden from man! . . . that heavenly nothingness! The bosom of Being does not speak to man, except in the guise of man. Truly, all being is difficult to prove; it is difficult to make it speak" (*Werke* VI, 43).

Thus humanity is mirrored in its attitude to prayer. Magic, revelationary religions, mysticism, humanist creed, agnosti-cism, atheism—all mirror, positively or negatively, this central phenomenon of faith, man's attempts at communion with the divine.

Judaism is concerned with prayer in a very special sense. While spontaneous, private prayer is universal, and ritual incantations the practice of primitive religions, the first non-sacrificial, non-priestly, community prayer service originated in post-biblical Judaism. Christianity and Islam adopted this institution, which was to spread over the entire inhabited earth. The early Christian liturgy, too, as well as the structure of the Church service, was patterned after the service of the Synagogue. In the words of Travers Herford, "In all their long history, the Jewish people have done scarcely anything more wonderful than to create the synagogue. No human institution has a longer continuous history, and none has done more for the uplifting of the human race." It may be in order to point to the major lines of the development of Jewish prayer.

The Story of Jewish Prayer

From its earliest beginnings, the most inclusive Hebrew term for prayer is *Tefillah,* the original meaning of which seems to be "the invocation of God as judge." (The English word "prayer" stems from the Latin verb *precare,* to beg, entreat.) A common Hebrew designation of worship is *Avodah,* service, a term taken from the Temple Service in Jerusalem. The Greek Bible renders *Avodah* by *leitourgia,* liturgy.

The biblical writings refer to a variety of prayer forms: invocation of the deity, the prayer of petition and of thanksgiving, of the confession of sins and the supplication for forgiveness, prayers that express humility and trust, and, finally, the hymn, or prayer of praise.

In ancient Israel, prayer was a response to particular situations in the life of an individual or in national history. The divine worship was centralized in the Temple in Jerusalem, with its order of sacrifices and its studied priestly rituals. Prayer as an expression of the religious life of a community seems to have originated in the Babylonian Exile, a period, lasting about half a century, between the era of the First and the Second Temples (586 to 538 BCE). In the meetings of the exiles, readings from the Scriptures seem to have been accompanied, or followed, by a brief community prayer. In the worship of the

Second Temple (516 BCE to 70 CE), sacrificial rites were combined with a liturgic service. But the real need of post-Exilic times, with their increase of religious individualism and democratization of religious life, could be met only by the institution of synagogues as centers of worship outside the official Temple. The transition from Temple to synagogue seems to have been effected by the so-called *Maamadot,* lay representatives of the people who, twice a year, attended the Jerusalem Temple service for one week while the section of the country they represented observed special worship assemblies.

Jewish tradition attributes the formulation of regular prayers and benedictions to the "Men of the Great Assembly," who, following the example of Ezra the Scribe (mid-fifth century BCE), are credited to have shaped the spiritual life of the Second Temple period. They were instrumental in establishing the basic form of Jewish prayer: "Blessed (or, praised) art thou, O Lord" (the *Berakhah*), a phrase which expresses both the personal element ("thou") and the hymnic quality of prayer. As a general rule, the *Berakhah* forms either the introduction, or the conclusion, of a prayer, or both. Quite ancient is the custom of reciting the "Hear, O Israel" sections (the *Shema,* Deut. 6:4-9, 11:13-21; Num. 15:37-41), preceded and followed by brief benedictions. Equally ancient is the group of prayers called, in its final form, *Shemoneh Esreh,* i.e., "eighteen" (later even nineteen) benedictions, or *Amidah* (to be recited while "standing"), or *Tefillah, the* prayer. In its original form this "Prayer of Benedictions" was composed of the first three and the last three sections; in elemental language it combines thanksgiving, supplication, and hymn. The middle portions, designated for weekdays, were replaced by different arrange- ments for the Sabbaths and the various festivals. An important component of the early synagogue service were selections from the biblical psalms, the reading from the Torah on the Sab- baths, festivals, fasts, and market days (Mondays and Thurs- days), and, on the sacred days, a homiletic exposition of Scriptural readings. In the period of the Maccabean uprising (mid-second cent. BCE), so it is assumed, a regular daily service was a fairly common practice.

Upon this simple foundation of worship an elaborate structure of divine service was erected. Especially when, with the fall of Judaea and the Second Temple (70 CE), the syna- gogue remained the chief medium of communal religious life. New prayers and recitations were added to express the hope for the rebuilding of Zion, the Messianic redemption, and the coming of the Kingdom of God. The proper hours for prayer, the proper conduct of the service, occupied the attention of the talmudic scholars. Though there was objection to a final fix- ation of the liturgy, and spontaneity and variation of expres- sion were encouraged, there grew an ever stronger trend toward uniformity of a service that called for three daily assemblies, morning (*Shaharit*), afternoon (*Minhah*), evening (*Maariv*), an additional morning prayer (*Musaf*) on Sabbaths and festivals, and a supplementary closing prayer (*Neilah*) on the Day of Atonement. In addition to the synagogue liturgy, prayers became a standard practice of home life and the life of the individual. Meals were introduced by a benediction and concluded by Grace, the beginning and the end of Sabbaths and festivals were marked by a prayer of Sanctification (*Kiddush*) and of Separation (*Havdalah*), respectively; the eve of Passover was the time for a home celebration with a special liturgy (*Seder*); every occasion of life, happy or sad, every experience (such as witnessing lightning, seeing a rainbow, a sage, or a king) was introduced into the realm of the sacred by the utterance of a benediction. "The whole of life," says Moritz Steinschneider, "became a divine service with interruptions."

With the conclusion of the talmudic period and the beginning of the Middle Ages a new development set in, which persisted for many centuries. Poets composed liturgic pieces (*Piyut,* plural *Piyutim,* from the Greek *poietes,* poet) to be inserted into the various sections of the original form of prayer, especially on the festivals, and, more significantly, on the Days of Awe. The *Piyut* elaborated on the major themes of the sacred days and on events in the history of biblical Israel, extolled the majesty of God and Israel's love for Him. In contradistinction to the simple, unmediated, even terse language of the original prayers, the *Piyut,* soon after its inception, employed new art forms, such as the stanza, rhyme, and skillful allusions to biblical and midrashic phrases. In Spain, the cultural contact with Islam engendered the adaptation to Hebrew poetry of Arabic poetic style, the acrostic, and various meters. Special melodies were used for the recitation of the *Piyutim.*

A liturgic poem on the theme of penitence and divine mercy was called *Selihah* (plural, *Selihot,* forgiveness). The

Selihah gave voice to the sufferings of exile, to martyrdom, to the transitoriness of life. Abraham's readiness to sacrifice his son (*Akedah,* the Binding [of Isaac]) was used as a symbol of the Jew's religious attitude. The medieval persecutions provided the Hebrew poets with ever new material for the composition of *Selihot.* Leopold Zunz, the historian of synagogal poetry, saw in the *Piyut* and *Selihah* a revival of the teachings of the prophets and the faith of the psalmist, the former's address to the many and the latter's taking refuge in the One. The synagogue perpetuated both. About the year 1200 most communities had made their selections from the vast treasure of poetic creations and, in the main, established the liturgical rite they wished to follow.

In contrast to the stationary pattern of prayers which established "a bond of union despite geographical dispersal, and a bridge across the ages linking the present to the past," the *Piyutim* constituted "an ever-changing element in the Jewish liturgy; they enliven with personal accent or local color the universal order of services. . . . Within the larger brotherhood of Israel, and the stock of prayers common to all generations, the medieval synagogue . . . essayed and effected a conciliation and concordance of two contrary but complementary necessities of all spiritual life, arriving at a remarkable synthesis of liberty and order, unity and diversity, permanence and change. The old and the new, the recent and the remote, the casual and the constant, blend to enrich and reinforce each other" (Shalom Spiegel, "On Medieval Hebrew Poetry").

From the talmudic era onward various forms of mysticism made their impact upon the synagogue and the life of prayer. A rich assembly of mystical hymns goes back to the third century, according to G. Scholem, and so does the *Alenu*-hymn, ascribed to the Babylonian master, Rav. The 12th-century Jewish mystics of Germany greatly intensified the search for the deeper meaning of prayer; their love of God and His creation is best documented in the "Hymn of Unity" and "Hymn of Glory" which conclude the traditional Sabbath morning service. From the *Zohar* (Book of Splendor, 13th cent.) comes the hymn "Blessed be the name," recited on the Sabbath in the Torah Service. The Safed group of mystics that rallied around Isaac Luria (16th cent.) considered prayer one of the central pursuits in life; life was to be a continual process of worship. The best known hymn of the period is *Lekha Dodi* (Come, my friend), which became a part of the Sabbath Eve liturgy. Hasidism (18th-19th cent.) revived the religious enthusiasm of the Lurianic Kabbalah and followed the pattern of its liturgy.

Codification of Liturgy and Prayer Books

The first attempt to survey Jewish prayers is the Palestinian Tractate *Soferim* (6th-7th cent.). The first important record of the liturgy and its rules is the *Seder* (Order of Prayer) of *Rav Amram,* Gaon (head) of the Academy of Sura, Babylonia (9th cent.); the first complete ritual is the *Siddur* of the religious philosopher Saadia, Gaon of Sura (9th-10th cent.). The *Mahzor Vitry* (about 1120) compiled in the school of Rashi, the commentator of the Bible and the Babylonian Talmud, and Moses

Maimonides' Code *Mishneh Torah* (1180) record texts of prayers and regulations for worship.

Historically, two major "rites" developed: the Palestinian and the Babylonian. The former, represented by Saadia's *Siddur,* was adopted in Germany, France, and Eastern Europe (the *Ashkenazic* usage). In other parts of Europe the following variations developed: the Greek order, in the Balkans; the Roman order, in Italy and some parts of Turkey. The Babylonian ritual, preserved in the *Seder Rav Amram,* became the order of prayer of Spanish and Portuguese Jewry (the *Sephardic* usage) and of the communities of the exiles after the expulsion from Spain and Portugal (end 15th cent.). This rite was, in the main, adhered to by the Yemenites. The communities of Provence form a bridge between the two major rites. Naturally, the migrations of the Jews brought with them mutations of liturgic usage. L. Zunz counted seventy-five different "rites"; modern research has discovered many more.

The first printed prayer book was of the Roman rite and appeared in 1486 in Soncino and Casalmaggiore. The first edition of an Ashkenazic prayer book was published in Italy about 1490, and of a Sephardic, in Venice, 1524. The best edition of the Ashkenazic festival prayer book, with a scholarly commentary, is the *Mahzor* of Wolf Heidenheim (Rödelheim, 1800); his pupil, Seligmann Baer, published a critical edition of the prayer book with a philological and literary commentary (*Seder Avodat Yisrael,* Rödelheim, 1868; new edition, Schocken, Berlin, 1937).

As early as the 16th century there appeared translations of

the prayer book into Italian, Spanish, and Judeo-German. The first translations into English appeared in London in 1738 and 1766.

Side by side with the official, congregational, prayer books there developed an extensive literature of private prayers for various occasions. The Talmud preserves many private supplications attributed to the sages and pious men of that age; some of these compositions were later introduced into the formal liturgy. There exist in manuscript form thousands of private prayers in Hebrew and Arabic from the Middle Ages. For the untutored, and especially for women who were not as closely bound by the formal liturgy as men, devotional prayers (*Tehinnot*) were composed in the vernacular. In these *Tehinnot* humble piety, intense devotion, and a spontaneous, impulsive, expression prevailed. A Judeo-German collection of private prayers appeared in 1552, in Venice; a famous early collection of *Tehinnot* was published in 1609, in Basel.

Closer contact with Western thought and ways of life acted as a divisive force in modern Judaism. From the beginnings of the 19th century, reformist movements attempted a more or less drastic adjustment of Jewish prayer to the spirit of the times. The first prayer of a German reform group appeared in 1818, the first English reform ritual in 1841. In the United States, the *Minhag America,* by Isaac M. Wise, was published in 1857. However, faithful adherents of historical Judaism helped to safeguard the continuity of the classical liturgy, which, though a product of changes and developments, appears to the observer as an organically composed structure.

The Meaning of Prayer in Judaism

Prayer is the most intimate expression of religious life. Theology, religious philosophy, the law and its interpretation: these areas call for intellectual discrimination, keen analytical powers, logic, precision. Pursuit of the subject may lead to an involved, rigid thought-system, to a minutely precise legal code, or to an elaborate commentary. All these are normal, natural developments in an advanced, classical religion. In contradistinction, prayer is religion in its pristine form. The worshipper is no longer the logical thinker, the systematizer, the scholar. These attributes become irrelevant. Nothing is left in him but his being human. He is just man. Man before God. In Jewish tradition, study is meant to be a mode of worship; worship, on the other hand, may become a subject of learned investigation. But the act of worship must remain this sacred encounter between a creature and its Creator. Prayer, therefore, permits us an insight into the religious life of the average man and woman, into what ultimately mattered to the learned man and the thinker, and into the elemental force that time after time regenerated both scholarship and scholar. The prayer book, more than any other work of the Hebraic tradition, points to the core of the Jewish faith: inwardness, the hallowing of God's name, love for God and fellow man, the power of "turning" (*Teshuvah*), the affirmation of the element of the personal in the world.

However, the humble word of prayer that attempted to span the void between the self of man and the Thou of God has generated rites, rituals, and a vast literature; it evolved institutional safeguards, rigidly adhered-to customs and usages. Like any other human creation, prayer, the liturgy, the synagogue, are imperiled by the forces of habit, convention, mechanization. Prayer may turn into routine, liturgy into external function, the synagogue into mere institution. To meet this danger, the devout throughout history took pains to keep alive the spirit of true prayer and the purity of worship.

Philo of Alexandria saw the essence of worship in the prayer for God's love; prayer, he stated, brings freedom to man's soul; only he who prays is fully alive. Hillel the Elder rebuked those whose prayer made them feel proud (Abot de R. Nathan II, 27). The Talmud calls prayer the "worship in the heart" originating in man's love of God (Taanit 2a). In his prayer a man should regard himself as standing in the presence of the divine (Sanhedrin 22a); before praying, he should purify his heart (Midrash Exodus Rabba XXII, 3). In the Midrash the Congregation of Israel says: "We are poor, we have no sacrifices to bring as a sin offering," to which God replies: "Take with thee words" (Hos. 14:3), meaning, words of the Torah. But Israel confesses: "We have no knowledge," whereupon God answers: "Pray before Me and I shall accept you" (Exodus Rabba XXXVIII, 4). The Midrash on Psalms thus interprets the words "For thee silence is praise" (Psalm 65:2): "Thou art silent, and I shall be silent, as it is said, 'Be silent to the Lord, and wait patiently for Him' (Psalm 37:7)." He who shouts in prayer belongs to those who are of little faith (Berakhot 24b). If the worshipper considers prayer a burden, or if he does not pray as one seeking mercy, or if he fails to introduce "something new" into his prayer, then his worship is considered to be a standardized, mechanical performance that loses its value (Berakhot 29b).

The medieval poet Solomon ibn Gabirol expressed the view that "the best worship is silence and hope." In emphasizing *Kavvanah* (devoutness, direction of the heart, concentration of mind) Moses Maimonides reiterates the talmudic attitude to prayer and presages the theories of succeeding centuries. In his *Mishneh Torah* he teaches: "Prayer without devotion (*Kavvanah*) is no prayer at all. . . . What is devotion? Freeing one's heart from all other thought and regarding oneself as standing in the presence of God." The 13th-century Bible commentator, Moses Nahmanides, writes in the epistle to his son: "When you pray, remove all worldly concerns from your heart. Cleanse your thoughts and think of the word before your mouth utters it. . . . Thus your prayer will be pure and devout, and acceptable before God."

The mystics worship in a vision of divine response: "When men declare the unity of the Holy Name in love and reverence, the walls of earth's darkness are cleft in twain, and the Face of the Heavenly King is revealed; there is light unto all" (*Zohar*). "The prayer of the poor," the mystics say, "is received by God ahead of all other prayers" (*Zohar*). Prayer "clothes man in a garment of holiness, evokes the light and fire implanted within him by his Maker, illumines his whole being, and unites the Lower and the Higher Worlds" (*Zohar*). The 16th-century code of Jewish law, the *Shulhan Arukh,* opens with these words: "Let man strengthen himself like a lion and arise in the early morning to render service to his Creator, as David said, 'I will awake the dawn.' " A 17th-18th century scribe, mystic, and mathematician, Jonah Landsofer, left this in his ethical testament: "Prayer is an aspiration for that purity of heart which shall inspire the service of God in love and reverence."

The works of the hasidic movement contain much insight into the meaning of Jewish prayer, and prayer in general. Israel the Baal Shem, the founder of Hasidism, interpreted the prayer of the Psalmist, "Cast me not off in the time of old age" (71:9), to mean: "Do not let my world grow old." Another passage in the Psalms (147:1), "For singing to our God is good," was taken by the Hasidim to imply :"It is good if man can so bring it about that God sings within him." Nahman of Bratzlav, the Baal Shem's great-grandson, stated: "Fear other than fear of the Lord prevents the joy of true prayer. Strive to overcome this fear through faith." And from the hasidic master Levi Yitzhak of Berditchev comes this note to the concluding words of Psalm 72: "All the hymns and prayers are a plea to have His glory revealed throughout the world. Once the world is, indeed, filled with it, there will be no further need to pray."

In our own century, Abraham Isaac Kook, Chief Rabbi of Palestine and foremost interpreter of classical Jewish prayer, comments: "Man uplifts all creation with himself in prayer, unites all beings with himself, uplifts and exalts the All to the source of blessing and the source of life." Also: "When we desire any object in prayer, our intention must be to remove darkness and evil from the world and to strengthen the goodness and light of the fulness of divine life." A contemporary thinker, Leon Roth, considers "the whole tradition of Judaism one continuous prayer to be taught the path of life which leads in joy to the presence of God," and Abraham Joshua Heschel defines "the philosophy of Jewish living" as "essentially a philosophy of worship."

Comprehension of prayer is, naturally, not confined to the religious thinker in the technical sense of the term. Being a universally human phenomenon, prayer may become a concern of any serious writer. Micah Joseph bin Gorion (1865-1921), secularist and follower of Nietzsche, meditated: "It is not you alone that pray, or we, or those others: all things pray, and all things exhale their souls. In all things . . . a prayer of the heart is instinctive. . . . Creation is itself a sort of prayer of the Almighty." Franz Kafka, who considered writing "a form of prayer," felt that "humility provides everyone . . . with the strongest relationship to his fellow man. It can do this because it is the true language of prayer, at once adoration and the firmest of contacts. The relationship to one's fellow man is that of prayer, our relationship to oneself that of striving: it is from prayer that one draws the strength for one's striving."

The variety of emphasis in Jewish prayer makes possible this extension of application from the specifically Jewish to the universally human. It is at once a reality (in the heart of the devout) and a symbol (in the heart of the poet). It presupposes both the person in his solitariness and the community; neither is to retreat for the sake of the other. Also, Jewish prayer is simultaneously prayer of Israel, prayer of man *qua* man, and, anticipating the future, prayer of humanity. In prophetic vision (Isa. 56:7) incorporated into the liturgy of the Days of Awe, the Temple of the future is to be "a house of prayer for all peoples."

The simplicity of heart which underlies prayer, the general attitude of faith and trust that characterizes classical Judaism, the will to introduce a sense of sanctity into time, space, life, thought—these qualities are rare in modern man. If not an outright unbeliever, modern man is a doubter; his scepticism is turned not only against God but, in equal measure, against himself; he lives in preliminaries, provisional positions, and rejects ultimates. He may, as a member of a group, "attend" a religious service, "go through" the ritual as a function vaguely associated with the life pattern of his inherited religion. Inhibited, curbed, often frustrated in his communication with fellow men beyond the technical, practical level, how is he to communicate with the source of life and consciousness, God? Yet, no less than his ancestors, modern man is cognizant of the element of the personal of which we spoke at the beginning. What to them was a certainty is to him a problem, and not an academic one. Unless he surrenders to the concept of a radically mechanical universe, the personal element will assert itself as a crucial issue in his life. The self may break through the walls of isolation, or emerge from its diffusion in the nameless, faceless totality of things, and find its way to the "thou" of the other being. It may stop right there. And yet, it may take the decisive next step towards the thou in whom the element of the personal is not provisional, or arbitrary, but abso-

lute. It may find itself alive in what has been called "a responding universe," a universe, too, that calls for man's response.
Then man may find himself at prayer. And he will discover
himself to be a member of a historic community which be-
lieved that a spark of meaning is hidden in the mass of seem-
ingly senseless affairs, and that chaos has been, and is constantly
being, overcome by the loving force of Creation.

N.N.G.

CREATION

You Are He Who Was

You are He who was
when the world was not created,
and you are He who has been
since the world's creation.

You are He who is
in this world,
and you are He
who shall be for the world-to-be.

Sacred make your name
through those that sanctify it,
and sacred make your name
in your world.
Then in your salvation may our horn rise high!

אתה הוא

אַתָּה הוּא
עַד שֶׁלֹּא נִבְרָא הָעוֹלָם
אַתָּה הוּא
מִשֶּׁנִּבְרָא הָעוֹלָם.

אַתָּה הוּא
בָּעוֹלָם הַזֶּה
וְאַתָּה הוּא
לָעוֹלָם הַבָּא.

קַדֵּשׁ אֶת שִׁמְךָ
עַל מַקְדִּישֵׁי שְׁמֶךָ
וְקַדֵּשׁ אֶת שִׁמְךָ
בְּעוֹלָמֶךָ.
וּבִישׁוּעָתְךָ תָּרוּם וְתַגְבִּהַּ קַרְנֵנוּ.

A Hymn on Creation

King of kings,

God of gods and Lord of lords

He who is surrounded with chains of crowns

Who is encompassed by the cluster of the rulers of radiance,

Who covers the heavens with the wing of His magnificence,

And in His majesty appeared from the heights,

From His beauty the deeps were enkindled,

And from His stature the heavens are sparkling.

His stature sends out the lofty,

And His crown blazes out the mighty,

And His garment flows with the precious.

And all trees shall rejoice in His word,

And herbs shall exult in His rejoicing,

And His words shall drop as perfumes,

Flowing forth in flames of fire,

Giving joy to those who search them,

And quiet to those who fulfill them.

מלך המלכים
אלהי האלהים ואדוני האדונים
המסובב בקשרי כתרים
המוקף בענפי נגידי נוגה
שבענף [ושבכנף?] הודו כסה שמים
ובהדרו הופיע ממרומים
מיופיו נתבערו תהומות
ומתארו נתזו שחקים
וגאים מפליט תארו
ואיתנים מפוצץ כתרו
ויקרים טורד חלוקו
וכל עצים ישמחו בדברו
וירננו דשאים בשמחתו
ודבריו יזלו בשמים
טורדין ויוצאין בלהבי אש
חדוה נותנין לשוחריהם
ושלוה למקיימיהם.

May the Name Send His Hidden Light

May the Name send his hidden light,
To open to his servants gates of aid,
To light their heart, numb, sunk in gloom of night.

May the great King bethink him, emerge in perfection and in
    right,
And open for us wisdom's gates,
And awaken love of old, and of ancient days.

האור הנעלם

יִשְׁלַח הַשֵׁם אוֹרוֹ הַנֶּעְלָם
לִפְתּחַ שַׁעֲרֵי עֶזְרָה לַעֲבָדָיו
וּלְהָאִיר לְבֵן נָתוּן בָּאֹפֶל וְנֶאְלָם.

יִתְעַשֵׁת הַמֶּלֶךְ הַגָּדוֹל יִצְדַּק וְיָשְׁלָם
וְיִפְתַּח לָנוּ שַׁעֲרֵי חָכְמָה
וִיעוֹרֵר אַהֲבַת קֶדֶם וִימוֹת עוֹלָם.

Who at His Word Makes Evening Fall

Blessed art thou, O Lord
our God, King of the universe,
who at his word makes evening fall,
in wisdom opens gates of heaven,
with comprehension changes tides;
who alternates the seasons,
who sets the stars at their stations
in the firmament at his will;

he who creates day and night,
rolls light before darkness,
darkness before light away;
who makes day pass, who brings night in,
who separates the night from day;
his name is Lord of hosts.

Blessed art thou, O Lord,
who makes evening fall.

בָּרוּךְ אַתָּה יְיָ
אֱלֹהֵינוּ מֶלֶךְ הָעוֹלָם
אֲשֶׁר בִּדְבָרוֹ מַעֲרִיב עֲרָבִים
בְּחָכְמָה פּוֹתֵחַ שְׁעָרִים
וּבִתְבוּנָה מְשַׁנֶּה עִתִּים
וּמַחֲלִיף אֶת הַזְּמַנִּים
וּמְסַדֵּר אֶת הַכּוֹכָבִים בְּמִשְׁמְרוֹתֵיהֶם
בָּרָקִיעַ כִּרְצוֹנוֹ.

בּוֹרֵא יוֹם וָלָיְלָה
גּוֹלֵל אוֹר מִפְּנֵי חֹשֶׁךְ
וְחֹשֶׁךְ מִפְּנֵי אוֹר.
וּמַעֲבִיר יוֹם וּמֵבִיא לָיְלָה
וּמַבְדִּיל בֵּין יוֹם וּבֵין לָיְלָה
יְיָ צְבָאוֹת שְׁמוֹ.

בָּרוּךְ אַתָּה יְיָ
הַמַּעֲרִיב עֲרָבִים.

Creator of Light

Bless ye the Lord to whom all praise is due.

Blessed be the Lord to whom all praise is due for ever and ever.

Blessed art thou, O Lord our God, King of the universe,
who formest light and createst darkness,
who makest peace
and createst all things.

Everlasting light is in His treasury of life;
He spoke and out of darkness there came light.

Blessed be His name and exalted the mention of the King
over kings of kings, the Holy One, blessed be He;
who is the Lord over all His creatures, ruler over all His deeds,
mighty above and below, there is none beside Him,
God in the heaven above and on earth below.
Therefore it is our duty to thank Him and to bless Him.

יוֹצֵר אוֹר

בָּרְכוּ אֶת יְיָ הַמְבֹרָךְ.

בָּרוּךְ יְיָ הַמְבֹרָךְ לְעוֹלָם וָעֶד.

בָּרוּךְ אַתָּה יְיָ אֱלֹהֵינוּ מֶלֶךְ הָעוֹלָם
יוֹצֵר אוֹר וּבוֹרֵא חֹשֶׁךְ
עֹשֶׂה שָׁלוֹם
וּבוֹרֵא אֶת הַכֹּל.

אוֹר עוֹלָם בְּאוֹצַר חַיִּים
אוֹרוֹת מֵאֹפֶל אָמַר וַיֶּהִי.

יִתְבָּרַךְ שְׁמוֹ וְיִתְעַלֶּה זִכְרוֹ שֶׁל מֶלֶךְ מַלְכֵי הַמְּלָכִים הַקָּדוֹשׁ
בָּרוּךְ הוּא
שֶׁהוּא אֲדוֹן כָּל בְּרִיּוֹתָיו שַׁלִּיט בְּכָל מַעֲשָׂיו
אַדִּיר בָּעֶלְיוֹנִים וּבַתַּחְתּוֹנִים וְאֵין זוּלָתוֹ
אֱלֹהִים בַּשָּׁמַיִם מִמַּעַל וְעַל הָאָרֶץ מִתָּחַת.
לְפִיכָךְ אֲנַחְנוּ חַיָּבִים לְהוֹדוֹת לוֹ וּלְבָרְכוֹ.

Shaper of Origins

Be it thy will,
O Lord my God and God of my fathers,
shaper of origins,
as thou hast called thy universe into being this day,
and thy unity proclaimed in thy universe,
and hast hung therein worlds above and worlds below
at thy word,

so with thy multiple compassion
unify my heart,
and the heart of all thy folk, Israel,
to love and to revere thy name.

And our eyes enlighten
in the light of thy Torah,
for with thee is the source of life:
in thy light shall we see light.

יוצר בראשית

יְהִי רָצוֹן מִלְּפָנֶיךָ
יְיָ אֱלֹהַי וֵאלֹהֵי אֲבוֹתַי
יוֹצֵר בְּרֵאשִׁית
כְּשֵׁם שֶׁהִמְצֵאתָ עוֹלָמְךָ בְּיוֹם זֶה
וְנִתְיַחַדְתָּ בְּעוֹלָמֶךָ
וְתָלִיתָ בּוֹ עֶלְיוֹנִים וְתַחְתּוֹנִים
בְּמַאֲמָרֶךָ

כֵּן בְּרַחֲמֶיךָ הָרַבִּים
תְּיַחֵד לְבָבִי
וּלְבַב כָּל עַמְּךָ בֵּית יִשְׂרָאֵל
לְאַהֲבָה וּלְיִרְאָה אֶת שְׁמֶךָ.

וְהָאֵר עֵינֵינוּ
בִּמְאוֹר תּוֹרָתֶךָ.
כִּי עִמְּךָ מְקוֹר חַיִּים
בְּאוֹרְךָ נִרְאֶה אוֹר.

Meditation Before the 'Sanctification'

God, it is true, before you there is no night, and the light is with you, and you make the whole world shine with your light.

The mornings tell of your mercy and the nights tell of your truth, and all creatures tell of your great mercy and of great miracles.

Each day you renew your help, O God! Who can recount your miracles? You sit in the sky and count the days of the devout, and set the time for all your creatures. Your single day is a thou-sand years and your years and days are unbounded.

All that is in the world must live its life to an end, but you are there, you will always be there, and outlive all your creatures.

You, God, are pure, and pure are your holy servants who three times every day cry, "Holy," and sanctify you in heaven and on earth:

You, God, are sanctified and praised. The whole world is filled with your glory forever and ever.

א תחינה פאר די קדושה

אס איז וואר גאט פר דיר איז קיין נאכט אונ' די ליכט רואט בייא
דיר אונ' דוא מאכסט דער לייכטן דיא גאנצי וואלט פון דיין
ליכט.

דיא מארגנט זאגן דיי'ני גנאד אונ' די נאכט זאגן דיין וואהרהייט
אונ' אלי קרעאטור זאגן דיי'ני גרוסי גנאד אונ' גרוסי וואונדר.

דו גאט דו טוסט דר ניי'אן דיא הילף אלי' טאג. ווער קאן דר צילן
דיין גרוסי וואונדר? דו זיצט אין הימל, דו צילסט די טעג פון דיא
צדיקים אונ' דו זעצט די צייט צו אלי' דיא בשעפניש אונ' דיין
איינציגר טאג איז טויזנט יאר אונ' דיי'ני יאר אונ' טעג די ווערן
ניט צו גרענצט.

אלז וואז אויף דער וועלט איז דאז ווערט פר לעבט אונ' דוא
בלייבסט אימר אונ' אייביג אונ' דוא איבר לעבסט אל דיי'ני
בשעפניש.

אזו וואול וויא דו ביזט ריין אזו זיין דיין הייליגי דינר ריין די אלי'
טאג דריי'א מאל זאגן קדושה אונ' טאן דיך הייליגן אויף דען
הימל אונ' אויף דר ערדן:

גהייליגט אונ' גלובט ביזטו גאט גפילט איז די גאנצי וועלט מיט
דיינר עהר אימר אונ' אייביג.

Meditation on the Creation of Man

Our God and God of our fathers, Creator of the whole world with your holy words. You are alone, there is none else, and so will you be forever in your oneness, and none will be there but you to rule this world and the world to come.

On this sixth day of the week, all of your holy thought was turned to creating man, who would rule all creatures below the heavens, on earth and on the sea, and would enjoy all the works which you have created for his sake upon the earth; so that man may at all times labor in your service to praise and to honor your holy name, to tell of your wonders and to point out the marvelous creations of your hands, how all the world is created in proper measure and number.

You have created man out of dust and have breathed a living spirit into his nostrils. With grace and mercy have you given him speech to praise your holy name. Such praise from man is more pleasing to you than the praises of all the angels in heaven, because man has permission to do either good or evil.

זאל זיין בוויליגט צו פר דיר גאט אונזר גאט, גאט אונזר עלטרן,
אונזר בשעפר, בשעפר פון די גאנצי וועלט פון אן פאנג די
וועלט מיט וואָרט דיינר היילִיקייט... דוא ביסט גוועזן אליין
אונ' קיינר מער אונ' צו אייביקייט וועדסטו זיין אליין אונ' איינ'יג
איינ'יגליך אונ' קיינר אוהן דיך צו רעגירן דיא וועלט אונ' יענר
וועלט.

היינט אן דען טאג איז אויף גאנגן דיא גדאנקן דיינר היילִיקייט
צו בשאפן דען מענש צו רעגירן אן אלי קרעטואר פון אונטר
דען הימל אויף ערדן אונ' אין דען וואסר אונ' צו גניסן אל דיין
בשעפניש דאס דו האסט בשאפן פון וועגן דען מענשן אויף די
ערדן דאס ער זאל זיין צו אלי צייט אין דיין דינסט צו לובן אונ'
צו עהרן דיין היילִיגן נאמן אונ' צו ערציהלן דיינֵי וואונדער אונ'
צייכן אונ' וואונדרליכי בשעפניש דיינר הענד וויא עז איז בשאפן
רעכטפערטיג מיט דער מאס איגזמיט דער צאל.

דוא האסט איהם בשאפן אויז דיא ערדן אונ' האסט איהם איין
גבלאזן איין אטם איין לעבנדיגן אין זיינֵי נאז לעכיר מיט גרוסר
גנאד אונ' באַרמהערציקייט דאס דוא האסט איהם געבן דיא
ריד אויס צו שפרעכן צו לובן דיין היילִיגן נאמן. זאלכי לוב פון
דען מענשן זיין דיר אן גנעם מער פון אלי די ענגיל אין הימל
אויז אורזאך דאס אים איז ערלויבט צו טון גוטס אודר ביז.

Blessing of the New Moon

Blessed is He whose utterance created skies,
the breath of His lips all of their host.

Law and time He fixed for them
that they alter not their function.

Joyous to do the will of their Master,
true Laborer, whose labor is truth.

And the moon He bade renew,
garland of glory for those borne from the belly,
destined like her to renew
and to glorify their Maker
for the honor of His kingdom.

Blessed art thou, O Lord,
who renews the moons.

קדוש לבנה

בָּרוּךְ אֲשֶׁר בְּמַאֲמָרוֹ בָּרָא שְׁחָקִים
וּבְרוּחַ פִּיו כָּל־צְבָאָם.

חֹק וּזְמַן נָתַן לָהֶם
שֶׁלֹּא יְשַׁנּוּ אֶת־תַּפְקִידָם.

שָׂשִׂים וּשְׂמֵחִים לַעֲשׂוֹת רְצוֹן קוֹנָם
פּוֹעֵל אֱמֶת שֶׁפְּעֻלָּתוֹ אֱמֶת.

וְלַלְּבָנָה אָמַר שֶׁתִּתְחַדֵּשׁ
עֲטֶרֶת תִּפְאֶרֶת לַעֲמוּסֵי בָטֶן
הָעֲתִידִים לְהִתְחַדֵּשׁ כְּמוֹתָהּ
וּלְפָאֵר לְיוֹצְרָם
עַל שֵׁם כְּבוֹד מַלְכוּתוֹ.

בָּרוּךְ אַתָּה יְיָ
מְחַדֵּשׁ חֳדָשִׁים.

A Perfect World

Blessed be He who did not let His world lack anything,

who created for it beautiful creatures,

and these beautiful trees,

that men may see them and be filled with joy.

שֶׁלֹּא חִסַּר בְּעוֹלָמוֹ כְּלוּם

בָּרוּךְ שֶׁלֹּא חִסַּר בְּעוֹלָמוֹ כְּלוּם
וּבָרָא בוֹ בְּרִיּוֹת טוֹבוֹת
וְאִילָנוֹת טוֹבִים
לְהִתְנָאוֹת בָּהֶם בְּנֵי אָדָם.

THE PRESENCE OF GOD

My Soul Thirsteth for Thee

O God, thou art my God, earnestly will I seek thee;
my soul thirsteth for thee,
my flesh longeth for thee,
in a dry and weary land, where no water is.
So have I looked for thee in the sanctuary,
to see thy power and thy glory.

For thy loving-kindness is better than life;
my lips shall praise thee.
So will I bless thee as long as I live;
in thy name will I lift up my hands.

For thou hast been my help,
and in the shadow of thy wings do I rejoice.
My soul cleaveth unto thee;
 thy right hand holdeth me fast.

צמאה לך נפשי

אֱלֹהִים אֵלִי אַתָּה אֲשַׁחֲרֶךָּ
צָמְאָה לְךָ נַפְשִׁי
כָּמַהּ לְךָ בְשָׂרִי
בְּאֶרֶץ־צִיָּה וְעָיֵף בְּלִי־מָיִם.
כֵּן בַּקֹּדֶשׁ חֲזִיתִךָ
לִרְאוֹת עֻזְּךָ וּכְבוֹדֶךָ.

כִּי־טוֹב חַסְדְּךָ מֵחַיִּים
שְׂפָתַי יְשַׁבְּחוּנְךָ.
כֵּן אֲבָרֶכְךָ בְחַיָּי
בְּשִׁמְךָ אֶשָּׂא כַפָּי.

כִּי־הָיִיתָ עֶזְרָתָה לִּי
וּבְצֵל כְּנָפֶיךָ אֲרַנֵּן.
דָּבְקָה נַפְשִׁי אַחֲרֶיךָ
בִּי תָּמְכָה יְמִינֶךָ.

From Eternity to Eternity

You are mighty forever, O God, valiant to all eternity, Lord
    over worlds without end.
The skies speak your bounty, your trust is on high.
Your valor is known to men, your glory to Israel.
Your psalms are sung from afar, the globe is full of your praises,
you who are Life of all life, for the life of the living is yours,
and you bring all to life with the four kinds of life that you made
    for the giving of life.

But first with the spirit of light, for the light of the spirit makes
    perfect the soul.
Then let the pillars of the great globe be measured, your praise
    shall not vanish!
For the mountains shall vanish, the reign of your kingdom is
    sure;
and the hilltops shall tremble and cease but not your compas-
    sion.

אַתָּה מָרוֹם לְעוֹלָם יְיָ גִּבּוֹר מִנִּי עַד וַעֲדֵי עַד מֵעוֹלָם וְעַד עוֹלָם
אַתָּה אֵל.

בַּשָּׁמַיִם חַסְדֶּךָ וֶאֱמוּנָתְךָ עַד שְׁחָקִים.

וְהוֹדַעְתָּ לִבְנֵי אָדָם גְּבוּרֹתֶיךָ וְעַל יִשְׂרָאֵל גַּאֲוָתֶךָ.

מִכְּנַף הָאָרֶץ זְמִירוֹתֶיךָ וּבְקַצְוֵי תֵבֵל מָלֵא שִׁבְחֶךָ.

וְאַתָּה הוּא חַיֵּי כָל הַחַיִּים הָעוֹלָמִים וְחַיֵּי כָל הַחַיִּים מִלְּפָנֶיךָ הֵם.

וְאַתָּה מְחַיֶּה אֶת כֻּלָּם בְּאַרְבַּעַת מִינֵי חַיִּים אֲשֶׁר הִתְכַּנְתָּ בָּהֶם
לְהַחְיוֹתָם.

בָּרִאשׁוֹנָה בְּרוּחַ הָאוֹר כִּי אוֹר הָרוּחַ נִשְׁמָתָם יִתֵּם.

וְיֵחָקְרוּ מוֹסְדוֹת תֵּבֵל מָתַחְתָּ וּתְהִלָּתְךָ לֹא תָמוּשׁ.

כִּי הֶהָרִים יָמוּשׁוּ לְבַל תָּסוּר מַלְכוּתֶךָ

וְהַגְּבָעוֹת תְּמוּטֶינָה וְלֹא יִכְלוּ רַחֲמֶיךָ.

Whosoever Knoweth Thy Name

Truly, whosoever knows thy name stands in awe of thee;

and whoever recognizes thee, mentions it with reverence, with
purity and with holiness.

For, in accordance with thy glory, thou didst conceal it from
the multitude of man,

entrusting it only to him who is meek, lowly of spirit, and
reveres thee; who is not prone to anger, and is great of heart.

Yet to every generation hast thou revealed a portion of the
mystery of thy Being.

כי כל אשר ידע את שמך

כי כל אשר ידע את שמך מפני שמך נחת הוא
והשומרו מזכירו ביראה ובטהרה ובקדושה.
כי לפי כבודך העלמתו מרב בני אדם
ואיננו נמסר אלא למי שהוא ענו ושפל רוח וירא שמים ואינו
כועס ואינו עומד על מדותיו.
ובכל דור סוד ממנו בארת.

With All My Strength

With all my strength and spirit, I adore
You, Truth, aloud and in my secret core.
I hoard your name. And who can rob this spoil?
He is my love. What other could I crave?
He is my light. How could my lamp need oil?
How can I falter, leaned on such a stave?
They mock—and do not know that mockery,
Because I praise your name, is praise to me.
Source of my life, your praise shall sound as long
As I can breathe my fervor into song.

בְּכָל לִבִּי אֱמֶת

בְּכָל לִבִּי אֱמֶת וּבְכָל מְאֹדִי
אֲהַבְתִּיךָ וּבְגְלוּיִי וְסוֹדִי.
שְׁמָךְ נֶגְדִּי וְאֵיךְ אֵלֵךְ לְבַדִּי
וְהוּא דוֹדִי וְאֵיךְ אֵשֵׁב יְחִידִי.
וְהוּא נֵרִי וְאֵיךְ יִדְעַךְ מְאוֹרִי
וְאֵיךְ אֶצְעַן וְהוּא מִשְׁעָן בְּיָדִי.
הֱקַלּוּנִי מְתִים לֹא יָדְעוּ כִּי
קְלוֹנִי עַל כְּבוֹד שִׁמְךָ כְּבוֹדִי.
מְקוֹר חַיַּי אֲבָרֶכְךָ בְּחַיַּי
וְזִמְרָתִי אֲזַמֶּרְךָ בְּעוֹדִי.

69

Lord, Where Shall I Find Thee?

Lord, where shall I find thee?
High and hidden is thy place;
And where shall I not find thee?
The world is full of thy glory.

I have sought thy nearness,
With all my heart I called thee,
And going out to meet thee
I found thee coming toward me.

יָהּ אָנָה אֶמְצָאֶךְ
מְקוֹמְךָ נַעֲלָה וְנֶעְלָם
וְאָנָה לֹא אֶמְצָאֶךְ
כְּבוֹדְךָ מָלֵא עוֹלָם.

דָּרַשְׁתִּי קִרְבָתְךָ
בְּכָל לִבִּי קְרָאתִיךְ
וּבְצֵאתִי לְקָרָאתְךָ
לְקָרָאתִי מְצָאתִיךְ.

Lord of the Universe... If You Had Cattle

Lord of the universe!

It is apparent and known unto you,

that if you had cattle and gave them to me to tend,

though I take wages for tending from all others,

from you I would take nothing,

because I love you.

אלו היה לך בהמות

רִבּוֹנוֹ שֶׁל עוֹלָם
גָּלוּי וְיָדוּעַ לְפָנֶיךָ
שֶׁאִלּוּ הָיָה לְךָ בְּהֵמוֹת וְנוֹתְנָם לִי לְשָׁמְרָם
לַכֹּל אֲנִי שׁוֹמֵר בְּשָׂכָר
וּלְךָ הָיִיתִי שׁוֹמֵר בְּחִנָּם
כִּי אֲנִי אוֹהֵב אוֹתְךָ.

Heart's Companion

Heart's companion, Father compassionate, draw thy servant
to thy will.
Hart-like may thy servant fleet, and before thy glory kneel.
Sweeter to him be thy favors than honey-of-comb and all fla-
vors.

Thou, resplendent in earth's glow, sick my heart is with thy
love.
I pray my God, heal, pray, my heart, and show my heart thy
pleasant glow.
Then shall it come into its strength, and healed shall know of
joy at length.

Thou Constant, thy compassions whelm, and pray guard thy
darling son.
It is so long now I have longed to witness of thy glory strong.
I pray my God, dear heart, pray spare and hold not thyself
apart.

Reveal thee, pray, and spread, my Friend, above my head thy
hut of peace.
Light thou on earth thine honor that we may delight and joy in
thee.
Haste thee, beloved, the tide has come. Be gracious as in ancient
days.

ידיד נפש

יְדִיד נֶפֶשׁ אָב הָרַחֲמָן מְשׁוֹךְ עַבְדְּךָ אֶל רְצוֹנֶךְ
יָרוּץ עַבְדְּךָ כְּמוֹ אַיָּל יִשְׁתַּחֲוֶה אֶל מוּל הֲדָרֶךְ
יֶעֱרַב לוֹ יְדִידוֹתֶיךָ מִנֹּפֶת צוּף וְכָל טָעַם.

הָדוּר נָאֶה זִיו הָעוֹלָם נַפְשִׁי חוֹלַת אַהֲבָתֶךְ
אָנָּא אֵל נָא רְפָא נָא לָהּ בְּהַרְאוֹת לָהּ נֹעַם זִיוֶךְ
אָז תִּתְחַזֵּק וְתִתְרַפֵּא וְהָיְתָה לָהּ שִׂמְחַת עוֹלָם.

וָתִיק יֶהֱמוּ נָא רַחֲמֶיךָ וְחוּסָה נָּא עַל בֵּן אֲהוּבֶךְ
כִּי זֶה כַּמָּה נִכְסוֹף נִכְסַפְתִּי לִרְאוֹת בְּתִפְאֶרֶת עֻזֶּךְ
אָנָּא אֵלִי חֶמְדַּת לִבִּי חוּסָה נָּא וְאַל תִּתְעַלָּם.

הִגָּלֵה נָא וּפְרוֹס חֲבִיבִי עָלַי אֶת סֻכַּת שְׁלוֹמֶךְ
תָּאִיר אֶרֶץ מִכְּבוֹדֶךְ נָגִילָה וְנִשְׂמְחָה בָּךְ
מַהֵר אָהוּב כִּי בָא מוֹעֵד וְחָנֵּנוּ כִּימֵי עוֹלָם.

Whom Have I in Heaven but Thee?

"Whom have I in heaven but thee?
Beside thee, I wish nought on earth.
My flesh is wasted and my heart;
the rock of my heart, and my portion
is God forever."

Master of the universe, Lord of all, thou whose dominion is
    everywhere,
for thou art the Place of the universe, not the universe thy
    place.
Give me a heart of truth, a virtuous heart and pure,
to do thee service and reverence,
a true heart of a Jew.

May I be worthy that my heart may be the dwelling of thy
    glory.
That there be drawn into my heart the presence of thy glory,
    great and sacred,
dwelling in the hearts of each and every one of Israel, thy sacred
    folk.
And everywhere I come, where I sojourn and where I journey
    according to thy will,
may I be worthy there to find thy divinity, truthfully;

מי לי בשמים

מִי לִי בַשָּׁמָיִם
וְעִמְּךָ לֹא חָפַצְתִּי בָאָרֶץ.
כָּלָה שְׁאֵרִי וּלְבָבִי
צוּר לְבָבִי וְחֶלְקִי
אֱלֹהִים לְעוֹלָם.

רִבּוֹנוֹ שֶׁל עוֹלָם אֲדוֹן כֹּל אֲשֶׁר בְּכָל מְקוֹמוֹת מֶמְשַׁלְתֶּךָ
כִּי אַתָּה מְקוֹמוֹ שֶׁל עוֹלָם וְאֵין הָעוֹלָם מְקוֹמֶךָ
תֵּן לִי לֵב אֱמֶת לֵב כָּשֵׁר וְטָהוֹר
לַעֲבוֹדָתְךָ וּלְיִרְאָתֶךָ
לֵב יִשְׂרָאֵל בֶּאֱמֶת.

עַד שֶׁאֶזְכֶּה שֶׁיִּהְיֶה לִבִּי מִשְׁכַּן כְּבוֹדֶךָ
שֶׁיִּהְיֶה נִמְשָׁךְ לְתוֹךְ לִבִּי שְׁכִינַת כְּבוֹדְךָ הַגָּדוֹל וְהַקָּדוֹשׁ
הַשּׁוֹכֵן בְּתוֹךְ לְבָבוֹת שֶׁל כָּל אֶחָד וְאֶחָד מִיִּשְׂרָאֵל עַמְּךָ הַקָּדוֹשׁ.
וּבְכָל מָקוֹם וּמָקוֹם שֶׁאָבוֹא לְשָׁם בַּחֲנָיָה וּבִנְסִיעָה כְּפִי רְצוֹנֶךָ
אֶזְכֶּה לִמְצֹא שָׁם אֱלֹהוּתְךָ בֶּאֱמֶת

77

and to near thee, and to cling to thee, truthfully.

Purify my heart to worship thee, truthfully.

"Unite my heart thy name to revere."

"A pure heart create for me, oh God,

and an upright spirit in me renew."

וּלְהִתְקָרֵב אֵלֶיךָ וּלְהִתְדַּבֵּק בְּךָ בֶּאֱמֶת.

טַהֵר לִבִּי לְעָבְדְךָ בֶּאֱמֶת.

יַחֵד לְבָבִי לְיִרְאָה שְׁמֶךָ.

לֵב טָהוֹר בְּרָא לִי אֱלֹהִים

וְרוּחַ נָכוֹן חַדֵּשׁ בְּקִרְבִּי.

The Song of "You"

Master of the universe, master of the universe,
Master of the universe, I'll sing you a you‑song.

You‑you‑you...

Where can I find you,
and where can I not find you?
You‑you‑you, you‑you...

It's—here I go—you,
and there I go—you,
still you, but you, only you, ever you—
You‑you‑you, you‑you!

East is—you, West is—you!
North is—you, South is—you!
You‑you‑you.

Sky is—you, earth is—you,
high up—you, deep down—you.
In every trend, at every end,
only you, you again, always you.
You! you! you!

א דודעלע

רִבּוֹנוֹ שֶׁל עוֹלָם, רִבּוֹנוֹ שֶׁל עוֹלָם
רִבּוֹנוֹ שֶׁל עוֹלָם, כוועל דיר א דודעלע זינגען.

דו – דו – דו.

אַיֵה אֶמְצָאֵךְ וְאַיֵה לֹא אֶמְצָאֵךְ.
וואו קאן איך דיך יא געפינען,
און וואו קאן איך דיך נישט געפינען.

אז – וואו איך גיי – דו,
און וואו איך שטיי – דו,
רק דו, נאר דו, ווידער דו, אבער דו –
דו – דו – דו, דו – דו.

מזרח – דו, מערב – דו,
צפון – דו, דרום – דו
דו – דו – דו.

שמים דו, ארץ דו
מעלה דו, מטה דו,
וואו איך קער מיך וואו איך וועגד מיך
רק דו, נאר דו, ווידער דו, אבער דו –
דו, דו, דו.

And Yet I Pray

Oh, thou my God: all peoples praise thee and assure thee of
their devotion.

But what does it mean to thee whether I do this or not?

Who am I, that I should believe my prayers are necessary?

When I say "God," I know that I speak of the Only, Eternal,
Omnipotent, All-Knowing and Inconceivable One, of
whom I neither can nor should make for myself an image;

on whom I neither may nor can make any demand; who
will fulfill my most fervent prayer, or ignore it;

and yet I pray as each one prays who is alive; and yet I pray for
mercies, miracles: fulfillments.

And yet, I pray, for I do not want to lose the blissful feeling of
unity, of communion with thee.

Oh, thou, my God: thy mercy left us prayer as a bond, a blissful bond with thee: a gift greater than any fulfillment.

Und trotzdem bete ich

O, du mein Gott: alle Völker preisen dich und versichern dich
ihrer Ergebenheit.

Was aber kann es dir bedeuten, ob ich das auch tue oder nicht?

Wer bin ich, dass ich glauben soll, mein Gebet sei eine Not-
wendigkeit?

Wenn ich Gott sage, weiss ich, dass ich damit von dem Einzi-
gen, Ewigen, Allmächtigen, Allwissenden und Unvor-
stellbaren spreche, von dem ich mir ein Bild weder machen
kann noch soll.

An den ich keinen Anspruch erheben kann oder soll, der
mein heissestes Gebet erfüllen oder nicht beachten wird.

Und trotzdem bete ich, wie alles Lebende betet; trotzdem er-
bitte ich Gnaden und Wunder; Erfüllungen.

Trotzdem bete ich, denn ich will nicht des beseligenden Ge-
fühls der Einigkeit, der Vereinigung mit dir, verlustig
werden.

O du mein Gott, deine Gnade hat uns das Gebet gelassen, als
eine Verbindung mit dir. Als eine Seligkeit, die uns mehr
gibt, als jede Erfüllung.

MY TIMES ARE IN THY HAND

I Trust in Thee

But as for me, I trust in thee,
O Lord,
I say, "Thou art my God."
My times are in thy hand;
deliver me from the hand of my enemies,
and from them that persecute me.
Let thy face shine upon thy servant,
save me in thy steadfast love.

עָלֶיךָ בטחתי

וַאֲנִי עָלֶיךָ בָטַחְתִּי
יְהוָה
אָמַרְתִּי אֱלֹהַי אָתָּה.
בְּיָדְךָ עִתּתַי
הַצִּילֵנִי מִיַּד אוֹיְבַי
וּמֵרֹדְפָי.
הָאִירָה פָנֶיךָ עַל עַבְדֶּךָ
הוֹשִׁיעֵנִי בְחַסְדֶּךָ.

Man's Way Is Not His Own

O Lord, I know that man's way is not his own;

it is not in man to direct his steps as he walketh.

O Lord, correct me, but in measure;

not in thine anger, lest thou diminish me.

לא לאדם דרכו

יָדַעְתִּי יְהֹוָה כִּי לֹא לָאָדָם דַּרְכּוֹ
לֹא־לְאִישׁ הֹלֵךְ וְהָכִין אֶת־צַעֲדוֹ.
יַסְּרֵנִי יְהֹוָה אַךְ בְּמִשְׁפָּט
אַל־בְּאַפְּךָ פֶּן־תַּמְעִטֵנִי.

What Is Man?

Let me alone; for my days are a breath.

What is man, that thou shouldst magnify him

and that thou shouldst set thy mind upon him,

that thou shouldst remember him every morning,

and try him every moment?

How long wilt thou not look away from me,

nor let me alone till I swallow down my spittle?

If I sin, what do I unto thee, thou watcher of men?

Why hast thou made me thy mark,

so that I am a burden to myself?

Why dost thou not pardon my transgression,

and take away mine iniquity?

For now shall I lie in the dust;

thou wilt seek me, but I shall not be.

חֲדַל מִמֶּנִּי כִּי־הֶבֶל יָמָי.

מָה־אֱנוֹשׁ כִּי תְגַדְּלֶנּוּ

וְכִי־תָשִׁית אֵלָיו לִבֶּךָ.

וַתִּפְקְדֶנּוּ לִבְקָרִים

לִרְגָעִים תִּבְחָנֶנּוּ.

כַּמָּה לֹא־תִשְׁעֶה מִמֶּנִּי

לֹא תַרְפֵּנִי עַד־בִּלְעִי רֻקִּי.

חָטָאתִי מָה אֶפְעַל לָךְ נֹצֵר הָאָדָם

לָמָה שַׂמְתַּנִי לְמִפְגָּע לָךְ

וָאֶהְיֶה עָלַי לְמַשָּׂא.

וּמֶה לֹא־תִשָּׂא פִשְׁעִי

וְתַעֲבִיר אֶת־עֲוֹנִי

כִּי־עַתָּה לֶעָפָר אֶשְׁכָּב

וְשִׁחַרְתַּנִי וְאֵינֶנִּי.

O Lord, Thou Lover of Souls

Thou hast mercy on all,

for thou canst do all things,

and thou overlookest the sins of men

because they should amend.

For thou lovest all things that are,

and abhorrest nothing which thou hast made;

for never wouldst thou have made any thing if thou didst hate

    it.

And how could any thing have endured, if it had not been thy

    will?

Or been preserved, if not called by thee?

But thou sparest all:

for they are thine,

O Lord, thou lover of souls;

for thine incorruptible spirit is in all things.

אֲדוֹן חֵפֶץ בַּחַיִּים

אַתָּה מְרַחֵם עַל־כֹּל
כִּי תוּכַל כֹּל
וְתַעֲלִים עַיִן מִפִּשְׁעֵי בְּנֵי אָדָם
לְמַעַן יָשׁוּבוּ.
כִּי אַתָּה אוֹהֵב כָּל־הַמְּצוּאִים
וְלֹא תְתַעֵב מְאוּמָה מִכָּל אֲשֶׁר עָשִׂיתָ
וְלֹא כוֹנַנְתָּ דָּבָר לוּ שְׂנֵאתָהוּ.
אֵיךְ יָקוּם דָּבָר וְאַתָּה לֹא חָפָצְתָּ
אוֹ אֵיךְ יַעֲמֹד וְאַתָּה לֹא פָקָדְתָּ.
אַתָּה תָחוּס עַל־כֹּל
כִּי לְךָ הוּא
אֲדוֹן חָפֵץ בַּחַיִּים
כִּי רוּחֲךָ הַקַּיָם לָעַד בַּכֹּל הוּא.

I Was Resolved to Do His Will

I was resolved to do His will—but how,
Since I was trapped in evil urge, and day
By day more hotly hastened to avow
Glib and pretentious words and idle play.

And surfeited with life, I slacked and moped,
The greed of owning soiled and dragged me down;
Deep in the slimy shaft of time I groped,
Unstaid, for I had swept through dams and bounds.

Speak! Do not turn to mute infinity!
Goad on my feet to find your law, compel
Me to obey, my Rock, what you ordain.

Oh, guide my going, smooth the path for me,
King of the world, and all my days I shall
Sing of your just and great and holy reign.

לעשות רצון קוני

לַעֲשׂוֹת רְצוֹן קוֹנִי אֱמֶת חָפַצְתִּי
מָה אֶעֱשֶׂה כִּי הַשְּׂאוֹר מוֹנֵעַ
גַּם הַזְּמָן מִיּוֹם לְיוֹם נוֹבֵעַ
בִּשְׂפַת חֲלַקְלַקּוֹת וְהִתְלוֹצַצְתִּי.

נִרְפֶּה אֲנִי נִרְפֶּה בְּחַיֵּי מָצְתִּי
כִּי בַעֲוֹן כִּתְמִי אֲנִי גוֹעַ
בְּיֵין מְצוּלוֹת הַזְּמָן טוֹבֵעַ
אֵין מַעֲמָד כִּי כָל־גְּבוּל פָּרָצְתִּי.

אַל תֶּחֱרַשׁ אַל תֶּחֱשֶׂה מִמֶּנִּי
תַּרְחִיב צְעָדַי אֶשְׁמְרָה חֻקֶּיךָ
צוּרִי וְתֶן חֶלְקִי בְּתוֹרָתֶךָ.

הַיְשַׁר לְפָנַי דַּרְכְּךָ וּנְחֵנִי
תָּמִיד לְשׁוֹנִי תֶּהֱגֶּה צִדְקֶךָ
מַלְכִּי וְכָל הַיּוֹם תְּהִלָּתֶךָ.

God, God of the Spirits

God, God of the spirits,
ruling in the worlds above and below,
put strength in me for thy service,
and for thy reverence and for thy Torah,
that in me the writ be fulfilled:
"At all times be thy garments white,
and be there no lack of oil on thy head."

And may I be a vessel prepared
to accept the soul, spirit, and breath
that thou hast breathed in me,
that I may in the future return
to the place whence thou hast hewn
my soul and my spirit and my breath.
May I be completely ready,
and be of those that are fortunate
"to behold the favor of the Lord,
and visit his habitation, all of which bespeaks his honor."
Amen.

אל אלהי הרוחות

אֵל אֱלֹהֵי הָרוּחוֹת
שַׁלִּיט בָּעֶלְיוֹנִים וּבַתַּחְתּוֹנִים
תֶּן בִּי כֹּחַ לַעֲבוֹדָתְךָ
וּלְיִרְאָתְךָ וּלְתוֹרָתֶךָ
שֶׁיֵּקִים בִּי מִקְרָא שֶׁכָּתוּב
בְּכָל עֵת יִהְיוּ בְגָדֶיךָ לְבָנִים
וְשֶׁמֶן עַל רֹאשְׁךָ אַל יֶחְסָר.

וְאֶהְיֶה כְּלִי מוּכָן
לְקַבֵּל נֶפֶשׁ רוּחַ וּנְשָׁמָה
אֲשֶׁר נָפַחְתָּ בִּי
כְּדֵי שֶׁאֶחֱזוֹר לֶעָתִיד
לַמָּקוֹם שֶׁחָצַבְתָּ
נַפְשִׁי וְרוּחִי וְנִשְׁמָתִי מִשָּׁם
וְלִהְיוֹת מוּכָן וּמְזֻמָּן
מֵאוֹתָם הַנּוֹחֲלִים
לַחֲזוֹת בְּנֹעַם יְיָ
וּלְבַקֵּר בְּהֵיכָלוֹ כֻּלּוֹ אוֹמֵר כָּבוֹד.
אָמֵן.

Thou and I

O God, my God,

Thou art the Master and I the servant.

Who should have mercy on the servant if not the Master?

Thou art God and I man.

Who should have mercy on man if not God?

Thou art the Living and I the dying.

Who should have mercy on the dying if not the Living?

Thou art the Potter and I the clay.

Who should have mercy on the clay if not the Potter?

Thou art the Deliverer and I the bound.

Who should have mercy on the bound if not the Deliverer?

Thou art the Holy and I the profane.

Who should have mercy on the profane if not the Holy?

Thou art the Shepherd and I the sheep.

Who should have mercy on the sheep if not the Shepherd?

Thou art the Listener and I the one who pleads.

Who should have mercy on the pleading if not the One who
    listens?

Thou art the Beginning and I the end.

Who should have mercy on the end if not the Beginning?

אתה ואני

אלהים אלי

אתה אדון ואני עבד

ומי ירחם על עבד הלא אדון.

אתה האל ואני אנוש

ומי ירחם על אנוש הלא האל.

אתה חי ואני מת

ומי ירחם על מת הלא חי.

אתה יוצר ואני חומר

ומי ירחם על חומר הלא יוצר.

אתה פותח ואני אסור

ומי ירחם על אסור הלא פותח.

אתה קדוש ואני חול

ומי ירחם על חול הלא קדוש.

אתה רועה ואני צאן

ומי ירחם על צאן הלא רועה.

אתה שומע ואני קורא

ומי ירחם על קורא הלא שומע.

אתה תחלה ואני סוף

ומי ירחם על סוף הלא תחלה.

Enable Us to Break Desire

Enable us to break evil traits and desire.

May we utterly negate ourselves until we arrive at true humility
like dust itself.

May we have the strength to attract your divine quality and
holiness unto ourselves,

and draw the entire world toward your holy faith, your true
saints, to serve you and your sacred law,

which you rendered to us through your prophet Moses and
through the true saints of each generation.

תְּזַכֵּנוּ לְשַׁבֵּר וּלְבַטֵּל כָּל הַתַּאֲווֹת הָרָעוֹת וְכָל הַמִּדּוֹת הָרָעוֹת

וְנִזְכֶּה לְבַטֵּל עַצְמֵנוּ לְגַמְרֵי עַד אֲשֶׁר נִזְכֶּה לַעֲנָוָה אֲמִתִּית בִּבְחִינַת עָפָר מַמָּשׁ.

עַד שֶׁנִּזְכֶּה שֶׁיִּהְיֶה לָנוּ גַּם כֵּן כֹּחַ הַמּוֹשֵׁךְ וְנִזְכֶּה לְהַמְשִׁיךְ אֱלֹהוּתְךָ וּקְדוּשָׁתְךָ אֵלֵינוּ

וּלְהַמְשִׁיךְ כָּל הָעוֹלָם כֻּלּוֹ לֶאֱמוּנָתְךָ הַקְּדוֹשָׁה וּלְצַדִּיקֶיךָ הָאֲמִתִּיִּים וְלַעֲבוֹדָתְךָ וּלְתוֹרָתְךָ הַקְּדוֹשָׁה

אֲשֶׁר גָּלִיתָ לָנוּ עַל יְדֵי מֹשֶׁה נְבִיאֶךָ וְעַל יְדֵי כָּל צַדִּיקֵי הַדּוֹר הָאֲמִתִּיִּים.

Humility

O Lord, thou only One, thou truly humble,

be it thy favor to make us worthy of perfect humility.

Such humility suggests life in the world-to-be and resurrection,

true and eternal life for every limb of the body,

complete absorption into the Infinite, blessed be He—

so that we may taste here on earth a life which suggests the
     world-to-be.

"I shall not die, but live, and declare the works of the Lord."

אָדוֹן יָחִיד הָעֲנָיו בֶּאֱמֶת

זַכֵּנוּ לַעֲנָוָה אֲמִתִּית כִּרְצוֹנְךָ הַטּוֹב

שֶׁנִּזְכֶּה לַעֲנָוָה בְּתַכְלִית הַשְּׁלֵמוּת

שֶׁעֲנָוָה כָזֹאת הִיא בְּחִינַת חַיֵּי עוֹלָם הַבָּא בְּחִינַת תְּחִיַּת הַמֵּתִים

בְּחִינַת חַיִּים אֲמִתִּיִּים וְנִצְחִיִּים שֶׁל כָּל אֵבֶר וָאֵבֶר

בְּחִינַת בִּטּוּל בֶּאֱמֶת אֶל הָאֵין סוֹף בָּרוּךְ הוּא

עַד שֶׁנִּזְכֶּה לִטְעוֹם גַּם בָּעוֹלָם הַזֶּה בְּחִינַת חַיֵּי עוֹלָם הַבָּא.

לֹא־אָמוּת כִּי־אֶחְיֶה וַאֲסַפֵּר מַעֲשֵׂי יָהּ.

Father of All Worldly Things

Father of all worldly things:
You create your world afresh each passing second,
and were you to withdraw your loving-kindness from creation
all would be as nothing in the twinkling of an eye.
But moment by moment you empty the vessels of blessing upon
    your creatures:
The morning stars appear again and sing you their love song
and the sun sallies forth boldly to sing its song of strength...
And the poor man cloaks himself again and bares his heart to
    you,
and again his soul's prayer cleaves your heavens as it ascends
    before you,
and again his body breaks beneath your terrible glory,
and again his eye is lifted toward you.
But one ray of your light and I abound in light,
but one word from you and I am reborn,
but one tremor of your eternal life and I am drenched in the
    dew of childhood.
O you who create all anew, O Father, create me, your child,
    anew.
Breathe in me the breath of your nostrils and I will live a new
    life, even a new life of childhood.

אבי כל באי עולם

אָבִי כָּל בָּאֵי עוֹלָם

אַתָּה בּוֹרֵא אֶת עוֹלָמְךָ בְּכָל־מְעוּף־עַיִן

אִם כְּהֶרֶף־עַיִן תָּסִיר אֶת חֶסֶד יְצִירָתְךָ וְהָיָה הַכֹּל אַיִן וָאָפֶס.

אֲבָל אַתָּה מֵרִיק עַל יְצִירֶיךָ צְנוֹרֵי בְּרָכָה בְּכָל־רֶגַע וָרֶגַע.

וְעוֹד פַּעַם יוֹפִיעוּ כּוֹכְבֵי־שַׁחַר וְשָׁרוּ שִׁירַת־אַהֲבָה לְפָנֶיךָ.

וְעוֹד פַּעַם יֵצֵא שֶׁמֶשׁ בִּגְבוּרָתוֹ וְשָׁר שִׁירַת־עֹז לְפָנֶיךָ . . .

וְעוֹד פַּעַם יַעֲטֹף עָנִי וְשָׁפַךְ אֶת־שִׂיחוֹ לְפָנֶיךָ.

וְעוֹד פַּעַם נִשְׁמָתוֹ־תְּפִלָּתוֹ בּוֹקַעַת רְקִיעֶיךָ בַּעֲלוֹתָהּ לְפָנֶיךָ.

וְעוֹד פַּעַם פּוֹר יִתְפּוֹרֵר גֵּוֹ מֵאֵימַת כְּבוֹדֶךָ.

וְעוֹד פַּעַם עֵינוֹ נְשׂוּאָה אֵלֶיךָ.

רַק קַו אֶחָד מֵאוֹרְךָ וְהָיִיתִי חֲדוּר אוֹרָה.

רַק דָּבָר אֶחָד מִדְּבָרֶיךָ וְקַמְתִּי לִתְחִיָּה.

רַק תְּנוּעָה אַחַת מֵחַיֵּי נִצְחֶךָ וְהָיִיתִי רְוּוִי טַל־יַלְדוּת.

הֲלֹא אַתָּה בּוֹרֵא הַכֹּל מֵחָדָשׁ בְּרָא־נָא אָבִי אוֹתִי יַלְדְּךָ מֵחָדָשׁ.

נְשֹׁם בִּי מִנִּשְׁמַת אַפֶּיךָ וְחָיִיתִי חַיִּים חֲדָשִׁים חַיֵּי יַלְדוּת חֲדָשָׁה.

Forgive Me

Forgive me, you whom we called by name,
You who appear, who shine beyond us.
I'm not to blame, not to blame
That my words are muddled and mumbled.

Many a time we endeavored to speak
To all your creatures—but they understood not.
Perhaps we weren't born in the desert council,
And he who was first—not our father?

For then when the radiant, reddish morn
First gored the eternity of the night,
My father too, my ancient father knew
How to bleat out his words as do rams to rams.

Then rain spoke to grass and thunder to lamb,
Then listened they all to Cain and Abel.
But what shall we do, what more shall we do,
We who utter our words to the void?

Forgive me, you whom we called by name,
Forgive me my words, my muddled soul.
I'm not to blame, not to blame—
Help me bleat to your creatures, as you do.

סְלַח לִי, אַתָּה שֶׁכִּנּוּךְ בְּשֵׁם,
אַתָּה הַנִּגְלֶה, הַזּוֹרֵחַ מִנֶּגֶד.
אֵינֶנִּי אָשֵׁם, אֵינֶנִּי אָשֵׁם,
כִּי שְׂפַת הַמִּלִּים נְבוֹכָה וְעִלֶּגֶת.

רַבּוֹת פְּעָמִים כְּבָר נִסִּינוּ דָבָר
אֶל כָּל יְצוּרֶיךָ, – אַךְ הֵם לֹא הֵבִינוּ.
אוּלַי לֹא נוֹלַדְנוּ בְּסוֹד הַמְדַבֵּר,
וְזֶה שֶׁהָיָה הָרִאשׁוֹן – לֹא אָבִינוּ?

כִּי אָז, עֵת הַבֹּקֶר, מַקְרִין וְאַדְמוֹן,
נִגַּח רִאשׁוֹנָה אֶת נִצְחוֹ שֶׁל הַלַּיִל
יָדַע גַּם אָבִי, גַּם אֲבִי הַקַּדְמוֹן,
לִגְעוֹת אֶת מְלָיו כְּמוֹ אַיִל אֶל אַיִל.

אָז גֶּשֶׁם אֶל דֶּשֶׁא וְרַעַם אֶל שֶׂה
דִּבְּרוּ וְהִקְשִׁיבוּ אֶל הֶבֶל וָמַיִן. –
אַךְ מַה נַּעֲשֶׂה עוֹד, מַה נַּעֲשֶׂה
אֲנַחְנוּ דוֹבְרֵי הַמִּלִּים אֶל הָאַיִן?

סְלַח לִי אַתָּה שֶׁכִּנּוּךְ בְּשֵׁם
סְלַח לְמִלַּי, לְנַפְשִׁי שֶׁנָּבוֹכָה.
אֵינֶנִּי אָשֵׁם, אֵינֶנִּי אָשֵׁם –
עָזְרֵנִי לִגְעוֹת לִיצוּרֶיךָ, כָּמוֹךָ.

DE PROFUNDIS

From the Depths I Called Thee

From the depths I called thee,
O Lord.
My Lord, heed thou my voice,
attentive be thine ears
to my pleading voice.
If, God, thou keep sins in mind,
my Lord, who would endure?
For thine is forgiveness
—wherefore art thou feared.

I have hoped, O Lord,
my soul has hoped,
and to his word have I aspired.
My soul goes out to my Lord,
more than the watchman to morning,
the watchman to morning.

Aspire, Israel, to the Lord
for with the Lord is mercy,
and with him much redemption.
And he shall redeem Israel from all his sins.

מִמַּעֲמַקִּים קְרָאתִיךָ
יְהוָה.
אֲדֹנָי שִׁמְעָה בְקוֹלִי
תִּהְיֶינָה אָזְנֶיךָ קַשֻּׁבוֹת
לְקוֹל תַּחֲנוּנָי.
אִם־עֲוֹנוֹת תִּשְׁמָר־יָהּ
אֲדֹנָי מִי יַעֲמֹד.
כִּי־עִמְּךָ הַסְּלִיחָה
לְמַעַן תִּוָּרֵא.

קִוִּיתִי יְהוָה
קִוְּתָה נַפְשִׁי
וְלִדְבָרוֹ הוֹחָלְתִּי.
נַפְשִׁי לַאדֹנָי
מִשֹּׁמְרִים לַבֹּקֶר
שֹׁמְרִים לַבֹּקֶר.

יַחֵל יִשְׂרָאֵל אֶל־יְהוָה
כִּי־עִם־יְהוָה הַחֶסֶד
וְהַרְבֵּה עִמּוֹ פְדוּת.
וְהוּא יִפְדֶּה אֶת־יִשְׂרָאֵל מִכֹּל עֲוֹנוֹתָיו.

The Lord Is My Shepherd

The Lord is my shepherd;
I shall not want.

He maketh me to lie down in green pastures;
He leadeth me beside the still waters.
He restoreth my soul;
He guideth me in straight paths
for His name's sake.

Yea, though I walk through the valley of the shadow of death,
I will fear no evil,
for thou art with me;
thy rod and thy staff, they comfort me.
Thou preparest a table before me in the presence of mine ene-
    mies;
thou hast anointed my head with oil;
my cup runneth over.

Surely goodness and mercy shall follow me
all the days of my life;
And I shall dwell in the house of the Lord for ever.

מזמור כ"ג

יְהֹוָה רֹעִי
לֹא אֶחְסָר.

בִּנְאוֹת דֶּשֶׁא יַרְבִּיצֵנִי
עַל מֵי מְנֻחוֹת יְנַהֲלֵנִי.
נַפְשִׁי יְשׁוֹבֵב
יַנְחֵנִי בְמַעְגְּלֵי צֶדֶק
לְמַעַן שְׁמוֹ.

גַּם כִּי אֵלֵךְ בְּגֵיא צַלְמָוֶת
לֹא אִירָא רָע
כִּי אַתָּה עִמָּדִי
שִׁבְטְךָ וּמִשְׁעַנְתֶּךָ הֵמָּה יְנַחֲמֻנִי.
תַּעֲרֹךְ לְפָנַי שֻׁלְחָן נֶגֶד צֹרְרָי
דִּשַּׁנְתָּ בַשֶּׁמֶן רֹאשִׁי
כּוֹסִי רְוָיָה.

אַךְ טוֹב וָחֶסֶד יִרְדְּפוּנִי
כָּל יְמֵי חַיָּי
וְשַׁבְתִּי בְּבֵית יְהֹוָה לְאֹרֶךְ יָמִים.

I Sat Alone Because of Thy Hand

Thou, O Lord, knowest;

remember me, and think of me, and avenge me on my persecu-

    tors;

take me not away because of thy long-suffering;

know that for thy sake I bear reproach.

Thy words were found, and I did eat them;

and thy words were unto me a joy and the delight of my heart;

because thy name was called on me, O Lord God of hosts.

I sat not in the assembly of merrymakers, nor did I rejoice;

I sat alone, because thy hand was upon me,

for thou hast filled me with indignation.

Why is my pain unceasing,

and my wound incurable,

so that it refuseth to be healed?

Wilt thou be unto me as a deceitful brook,

as waters that fail?

מפני ידך בדד ישבתי

אַתָּה יָדַעְתָּ יְהוָה
זָכְרֵנִי וּפָקְדֵנִי וְהִנָּקֶם לִי מֵרֹדְפַי
אַל־לְאֶרֶךְ אַפְּךָ תִּקָּחֵנִי
דַּע שְׂאֵתִי עָלֶיךָ חֶרְפָּה.
נִמְצְאוּ דְבָרֶיךָ וָאֹכְלֵם
וַיְהִי דְבָרְךָ לִי לְשָׂשׂוֹן וּלְשִׂמְחַת לְבָבִי
כִּי־נִקְרָא שִׁמְךָ עָלַי יְהוָה אֱלֹהֵי צְבָאוֹת.
לֹא־יָשַׁבְתִּי בְסוֹד־מְשַׂחֲקִים וָאֶעְלֹז
מִפְּנֵי יָדְךָ בָּדָד יָשַׁבְתִּי
כִּי־זַעַם מִלֵּאתָנִי.
לָמָּה הָיָה כְאֵבִי נֶצַח
וּמַכָּתִי אֲנוּשָׁה
מֵאֲנָה הֵרָפֵא
הָיוֹ תִהְיֶה לִי כְּמוֹ אַכְזָב
מַיִם לֹא נֶאֱמָנוּ.

In My Straits I Called

In my straits I called to the Lord,

and he did reply.

From the belly of the chasm, I screamed;

thou didst heed my voice.

When thou cast me deep into the heart of seas,

when the torrent surrounded me,

when all thy breakers and waves

passed over me—

Then I said, 'I am banished from before thine eyes.'

Yet shall I look again

toward thy sacred habitation.

The waters compassed me to the soul,

the deep surrounded me,

weeds wrapped round my head—

when I sank to the ends of the hills,

the earth, whose bars were about me forever—

thou raised me alive out of the pit,

O Lord my God.

When my soul fainted within me,

I recalled the Lord.

And my prayer came to thee,

תפלת יונה

קָרָאתִי מִצָּרָה לִי אֶל־יְהוָה
וַיַּעֲנֵנִי
מִבֶּטֶן שְׁאוֹל שִׁוַּעְתִּי
שָׁמַעְתָּ קוֹלִי.

וַתַּשְׁלִיכֵנִי מְצוּלָה בִּלְבַב יַמִּים
וְנָהָר יְסֹבְבֵנִי
כָּל־מִשְׁבָּרֶיךָ וְגַלֶּיךָ
עָלַי עָבָרוּ.

וַאֲנִי אָמַרְתִּי נִגְרַשְׁתִּי מִנֶּגֶד עֵינֶיךָ
אַךְ אוֹסִיף לְהַבִּיט
אֶל־הֵיכַל קָדְשֶׁךָ.

אֲפָפוּנִי מַיִם עַד־נֶפֶשׁ
תְּהוֹם יְסֹבְבֵנִי
סוּף חָבוּשׁ לְרֹאשִׁי.
לְקִצְבֵי הָרִים יָרַדְתִּי
הָאָרֶץ בְּרִחֶיהָ בַעֲדִי לְעוֹלָם
וַתַּעַל מִשַּׁחַת חַיַּי
יְהוָה אֱלֹהָי.

בְּהִתְעַטֵּף עָלַי נַפְשִׁי
אֶת־יְהוָה זָכָרְתִּי
וַתָּבוֹא אֵלֶיךָ תְּפִלָּתִי

to thy sacred habitation.

They who preserve their vain follies

their own mercy they desert.

And I, with a thankful voice, will sacrifice to thee.

What I pledged I shall fulfill;

salvation is the Lord's.

אֶל־הֵיכַל קָדְשֶׁךָ.
מְשַׁמְּרִים הַבְלֵי־שָׁוְא
חַסְדָּם יַעֲזֹבוּ.

וַאֲנִי בְּקוֹל תּוֹדָה אֶזְבְּחָה־לָּךְ
אֲשֶׁר נָדַרְתִּי אֲשַׁלֵּמָה
יְשׁוּעָתָה לַיהוָה.

Thou Hast Helped Me to Salvation

I thank thee, O God, for thou hast helped me to salvation;

hast not counted me with sinners for doom.

O God, remove not thy mercy from me,

nor thy remembrance from my heart until I die.

Establish the works of my hands before thee

and guard my steps in remembering thee.

Clothe my tongue and lips with words of truth;

anger and unreasoning wrath put far from me.

With goodwill and mercy support my heart;

when thou strengthenest my soul, what is given to me will

    suffice.

סמכתני לישועה

אוֹדְךָ אֱלֹהִים כִּי סְמַכְתַּנִי לִישׁוּעָה
וְלֹא מְנִיתַנִי עִם הַפּוֹשְׁעִים לַשָּׁחַת.
אַל־תָּסַר חַסְדְּךָ מִמֶּנִּי אֱלֹהִים
וְאֶת־זִכְרְךָ מִלִּבִּי עַד־מָוֶת.
מַעֲשֵׂי יָדַי כּוֹנְנָה לְפָנֶיךָ
וּפְעָמַי שְׁמֹר בְּזִכְרוֹנֶךָ.
לְשׁוֹנִי וּשְׂפָתַי הַלְבִּישָׁה דִבְרֵי־אֱמֶת
עֶבְרָה וְחֵמָה בְּעֶרְבָה הַרְחִיקָה מִמֶּנִּי.
בְּחֵן וָחֶסֶד סְמֹךְ לִבִּי
בְּאַמְּצְךָ נַפְשִׁי דַּי־לִי הַמַּתָּן.

The World Lies in Darkness

Let me speak before thee, O Lord!

The world lies in darkness,

and the dwellers therein are without light.

For thy law is burnt;

and so no man knows the things which have been done by
     thee,

or the works that shall be done.

If then, I have found favor before thee,

send unto me the Holy Spirit

that I may write all that has happened in the world since the
     beginning,

even the things which were written in thy law,

in order that men may be able to find the path,

and that they who would live at the last,

may live.

תבל שומה בחשך

אֲדַבְּרָה־נָא לְפָנֶיךָ אֲדֹנָי.
תֵּבֵל שׁוּמָה בַחשֶׁךְ
וְיוֹשְׁבֶיהָ בְּלִי אוֹרָה.
כִּי תוֹרָתְךָ נִשְׂרָפָה
וְעַל כֵּן אֵין־אִישׁ יוֹדֵעַ אֶת־אֲשֶׁר עָשִׂיתָ
וְאֵת־אֲשֶׁר יֵעָשֶׂה.
וְאִם־נָא מָצָאתִי חֵן בְּעֵינֶיךָ
תֶּן־בִּי רוּחַ קָדְשֶׁךָ
וְכָתַבְתִּי אֵת־אֲשֶׁר נַעֲשָׂה בָעוֹלָם מֵרֹאשׁ
אֲשֶׁר הָיָה כָתוּב בְּתוֹרָתֶךָ
לְמַעַן יוּכְלוּ בְּנֵי־אָדָם לִמְצֹא נְתִיבָה
אֲשֶׁר יַחְפְּצוּ לִחְיוֹת בַּיָּמִים הַבָּאִים
יִחְיוּ.

Hear Our Voice

Hear our voice, O Lord our God,
have mercy and compassion on us,
and receive compassionately, and acceptingly,
this our prayer.

Return us, O Lord, to thee, and we shall return;
renew our days as of old.

Hear our speech, O Lord,
our meditation comprehend.

Cast us not from before thee,
and thy holy spirit take not from us.

No, cast us not away, when we grow old;
when our strength expires forsake us not.

Forsake us not, O Lord our God;
be not far from us.

For to thee, O Lord, have we aspired;
thou shalt reply,
O Lord our God.

שמע קולנו

שְׁמַע קוֹלֵנוּ יְיָ אֱלֹהֵינוּ
חוּס וְרַחֵם עָלֵינוּ
וְקַבֵּל בְּרַחֲמִים וּבְרָצוֹן
אֶת תְּפִלָּתֵנוּ.

הֲשִׁיבֵנוּ יְיָ אֵלֶיךָ וְנָשׁוּבָה
חַדֵּשׁ יָמֵינוּ כְּקֶדֶם.

אֲמָרֵינוּ הַאֲזִינָה יְיָ
בִּינָה הֲגִיגֵנוּ.

אַל תַּשְׁלִיכֵנוּ מִלְּפָנֶיךָ
וְרוּחַ קָדְשְׁךָ אַל תִּקַּח מִמֶּנּוּ.

אַל תַּשְׁלִיכֵנוּ לְעֵת זִקְנָה
כִּכְלוֹת כֹּחֵנוּ אַל תַּעַזְבֵנוּ.

אַל תַּעַזְבֵנוּ יְיָ אֱלֹהֵינוּ
אַל תִּרְחַק מִמֶּנּוּ.

כִּי לְךָ יְיָ הוֹחָלְנוּ
אַתָּה תַעֲנֶה
אֲדֹנָי אֱלֹהֵינוּ.

125

The Gates of Mercy

Our eternal Savior, the King of gods, who alone art almighty,
and the Lord, and God of all beings, and the God of our
holy and blameless fathers, and of those before us;

the God of Abraham, and of Isaac, and of Jacob;

who art merciful and compassionate, long-suffering, and abundant in mercy;

to whom every heart is naked, and by whom every heart is seen,
and to whom every secret thought is revealed:

to thee do the souls of the righteous cry aloud,

upon thee do the hopes of the godly trust, thou Father of the
blameless, thou hearer of the supplication of those that call
upon thee with uprightness,

and who knowest the supplications that are not uttered:

for thy providence reaches as far as the inmost parts of man:

and by thy knowledge thou searchest the thoughts of everyone,

and in every region of the whole earth the incense of prayer and
supplication is sent up to thee.

O thou who hast appointed this present world as a racecourse
in righteousness,

and hast opened to all the gates of mercy,

and hast demonstrated to every man by implanted knowledge,
and natural judgment, and the admonitions of the law,

that the possession of riches is not everlasting, the ornament of

    beauty is not perpetual, our strength and force are easily

    dissolved;

and all is vapor and vanity;

and only the good conscience of faith unfeigned passes through

    the midst of the heavens,

and returning with truth, takes hold of the right hand of the

    joy which is to come.

And withal, before the promise of regeneration is accomplished

the soul itself exults in hope, and is joyful.

For from the beginning when our forefather Abraham laid

    claim to the way of truth

thou didst guide him by a vision,

and didst teach him what kind of state this world is;

and gnosis was the forerunner of his faith;

and faith was the consequence of his gnosis.

For thou didst say:

"I will make thy seed as the stars of heaven,

and as the sand which is by the sea-shore."

O thou great protector of the posterity of Abraham,

be thou blessed forever.

The God of Them That Repent

Thou, O Lord, according to thy great goodness hast promised
    repentance to them that have sinned against thee:
of thine infinite mercies hast appointed repentance unto sinners,
that they may be saved.
Thou, therefore, O Lord, that art the God of the just,
hast not appointed repentance to the just, as to Abraham, and
    Isaac, and Jacob, which have not sinned against thee;
but thou hast appointed repentance unto me that am a sinner.

I have sinned, O Lord, I have sinned,
and I acknowledge mine iniquities;
wherefore, I humbly beseech thee,
forgive me, O Lord, forgive me,
and destroy me not with mine iniquities.
Be not angry with me for ever,
by reserving evil for me;
neither condemn me into the lower parts of the earth.
For thou, O Lord, art the God of them that repent;
and in me thou wilt show all thy goodness;
for thou wilt save me, unworthy that I am,
according to thy great mercy.
Therefore I will praise thee for ever all the days of my life:
for all the host of heaven doth praise thee,
and thine is the glory for ever and ever. Amen.

אלהי השבים

אַתָּה יְיָ בְּרֹב טוּבְךָ הִבְטַחְתָּ סְלִיחָה לַחֹטְאִים
וּבְרַחֲמֶיךָ הָרַבִּים שַׂמְתָּ דֶּרֶךְ־תְּשׁוּבָה לָרְשָׁעִים
לְמַעַן יִוָּשֵׁעוּ.
אַתָּה יְיָ אֱלֹהֵי הַצַּדִּקוֹת
לֹא שַׂמְתָּ נֹחַם לְאַבְרָהָם לְיִצְחָק וּלְיַעֲקֹב הַצַּדִּיקִים שֶׁהֵם לֹא
חָטְאוּ לָךְ
כִּי אִם־לִי אֲנִי הַחוֹטֵא שַׂמְתָּ נֹחַם כִּי חָטָאתִי.

חָטָאתִי יְיָ חָטָאתִי

וּפְשָׁעַי אֲנִי אֵדָע.

וּבְכֵן אֶתְחַנֵּן אֵלֶיךָ

יְיָ סְלַח־נָא סְלַח לִי

וְאַל אֶסָּפֶה בְחַטֹּאתִי

וְאַל תִּטֹּר לְעוֹלָם

וְאַל תִּשְׁמָר־לִי עֲוֹנוֹת

וְאַל תַּשְׁלִיכֵנִי מִלְּפָנֶיךָ בְּתַחְתִּיּוֹת אָרֶץ

כִּי אַתָּה יְיָ אֱלֹהֵי הַשָּׁבִים אָתָּה.

הַרְאֵינִי־נָא אֶת־טוּבְךָ גַּם־אָנִי

וְהוֹשִׁיעֵנִי בְּרֹב רַחֲמֶיךָ

אַף כִּי אֵינֶנִּי רָאוּי.

וַאֲנִי אֲהַלֶּלְךָ תָמִיד כָּל־יְמֵי חַיָּי

כִּי אוֹתְךָ יְהַלְלוּ כָּל־צְבָא הַשָּׁמַיִם

וּלְךָ יְיָ הַכָּבוֹד לְעוֹלָם וָעֶד אָמֵן.

Let Me Return

You know the thoughts of men,

and read the minds of mortals.

You know that with all my heart

I desire to serve you.

Cleanse my mind and purify my thoughts from the vanities of

the world,

and save me from all forms of trouble and distress

that would put a barrier between me and you,

and would shut me out from your service.

Remove from my shoulder every man-made burden,

and make me single-hearted to bear the yoke of your command-

ments,

for by them my spirit lives.

Let me then return to you with all my heart in perfect repent-

ance.

"Create for me a clean heart, O God, and put a new steadfast

spirit in me."

אשוב אליך

אַתָּה הַיּוֹדֵעַ מַחְשְׁבוֹת אָדָם

וּמֵבִין סְעִפֵּי לֵב בָּשָׂר וָדָם

יָדַעְתָּ כִּי בְכָל־לִבִּי לַעֲשׂוֹת רְצוֹנְךָ חָפָצְתִּי.

הָבֵר מַחְשְׁבוֹתַי וְטַהֵר רַעְיוֹנַי מֵהַבְלֵי הָעוֹלָם

וְהַצִּילֵנִי מִכָּל־צָרוֹת וְצוּקוֹת

הַמַּבְדִּילוֹת בֵּינִי לְבֵינֶיךָ

וְהַמַּדִּיחוֹת אוֹתִי מֵעֲבוֹדָתֶךָ.

הַעֲבֵר סֵבֶל אֱנוֹשׁ מֵעַל־צַוָּארִי

וְיַחֵד לִבִּי לַעֲמֹס עַל מִצְוֹתֶיךָ

כִּי בָם חַיֵּי רוּחִי.

וְאָשׁוּב אֵלֶיךָ בִּתְשׁוּבָה שְׁלֵמָה בְּכָל־לִבִּי.

לֵב טָהוֹר בְּרָא לִי אֱלֹהִים

וְרוּחַ נָכוֹן חַדֵּשׁ בְּקִרְבִּי.

Give Me a Good Heart

May it please thee, O Lord my God and God of my fathers,
    that thy law should be my daily occupation.

And give me a good heart, and a good portion in life, and a
    good friend, and a humble soul, and a lowly spirit.

And let not thy name be profaned because of me, nor make me
    a byword in the mouths of thy creatures.

And let not my end be untimely death, nor let my hope turn in-
    to soul's despair.

And let me not be in need of the charity of creatures of flesh and
    blood, for their charity is small, while the humiliation is
    great; rather let me depend upon thy bountiful hand.

And make my portion in thy law together with those who do
    thy will with a perfect heart.

And rebuild thy Temple, thy city, thy palace, and thy sanctu-
    ary, soon and in our own days.

And hasten to answer me, and redeem me from all hard and
    evil decrees.

And save me in thy abundant mercy from all afflictions and
    trials.

For thou hearest the prayer of every mouth.

Blessed art thou, O Lord, who hearest all prayer.

תֵּן לִי לֵב טוֹב

יְהִי רָצוֹן מִלְּפָנֶיךָ יְיָ אֱלֹהַי וֵאלֹהֵי אֲבֹתַי שֶׁתְּהֵא תּוֹרָתְךָ אֻמָּנוּתִי.

וְתִתֶּן לִי לֵב טוֹב וְחֵלֶק טוֹב וְחָבֵר טוֹב וְנֶפֶשׁ שְׁפָלָה וְרוּחַ נְמוּכָה.

וְאַל יִתְחַלֵּל שִׁמְךָ בִּי וְאַל תַּעֲשֵׂנִי שִׂיחָה בְּפִי הַבְּרִיּוֹת.

וְאַל תְּהִי אַחֲרִיתִי לְהַכְרִית וְתִקְוָתִי לְמַפַּח נָפֶשׁ.

וְאַל תַּצְרִיכֵנִי לִידֵי מַתְּנַת בָּשָׂר וָדָם שֶׁמַּתְּנָתָם מְעוּטָה וְחֶרְפָּתָם מְרֻבָּה אֶלָּא לְיָדְךָ הַמְּלֵאָה וְהָרְחָבָה.

וְתֵן חֶלְקִי בְּתוֹרָתֶךָ עִם עוֹשֵׂי רְצוֹנֶךָ בְּלֵבָב שָׁלֵם.

וּבְנֵה בֵּיתְךָ עִירְךָ וְהֵיכָלָךְ וּמִקְדָּשְׁךָ בִּמְהֵרָה בְיָמֵינוּ.

וּמַהֵר עֲנֵנִי וּפְדֵנִי מִכָּל גְּזֵרוֹת קָשׁוֹת וְרָעוֹת.

וְהוֹשִׁיעֵנִי בְּרַחֲמֶיךָ הָרַבִּים מִכָּל צָרָה וְצוּקָה

כִּי אַתָּה שׁוֹמֵעַ תְּפִלַּת כָּל פֶּה.

בָּרוּךְ אַתָּה יְיָ שׁוֹמֵעַ תְּפִלָּה.

Do Your Will

Do your will in the heavens above,

and give tranquility of spirit to those in awe of you below;

and whatever is good in your eyes, do.

עשה רצונך

עֲשֵׂה רְצוֹנְךָ בַּשָּׁמַיִם מִמַּעַל
וְתֵן נַחַת רוּחַ לִירֵאֶיךָ מִתַּחַת
וְהַטוֹב בְּעֵינֶיךָ עֲשֵׂה.

THANKSGIVING

The Soul You Have Placed in Me

My God,

the soul you have placed in me

is pure.

You it was who created it,

you formed it,

you blew it into me,

you guard it within me,

you will take it from me,

and return it to me, in time-to-be.

All that time the soul is within me

I give thanks before thee,

O Lord my God and God of my fathers,

Master of all made things,

Lord of all the souls.

אלהי נשמה

אֱלֹהַי
נְשָׁמָה שֶׁנָּתַתָּ בִּי
טְהוֹרָה הִיא
אַתָּה בְרָאתָהּ
אַתָּה יְצַרְתָּהּ
אַתָּה נְפַחְתָּהּ בִּי
וְאַתָּה מְשַׁמְּרָהּ בְּקִרְבִּי
וְאַתָּה עָתִיד לִטְּלָהּ מִמֶּנִּי
וּלְהַחֲזִירָהּ בִּי לֶעָתִיד לָבֹא.

כָּל זְמַן שֶׁהַנְּשָׁמָה בְקִרְבִּי
מוֹדֶה אֲנִי לְפָנֶיךָ
יְיָ אֱלֹהַי וֵאלֹהֵי אֲבוֹתַי
רִבּוֹן כָּל הַמַּעֲשִׂים
אֲדוֹן כָּל הַנְּשָׁמוֹת.

139

Grace after Meals

Blessed art thou, O Lord our God, King of the universe,
who in his goodness feeds the whole wide universe, in grace, in
    mercy and in kindness.
He gives food to all flesh, for his mercy endures forever.

And because of his great goodness, we have never lacked food,
    and may we never suffer want of it, for the sake of his great
    name.
For he feeds and tends the universe; he does good to the world,
    and provides food for all the creatures he has wrought.

Blessed art thou, O Lord,
who feeds all living things.

בָּרוּךְ אַתָּה יְיָ אֱלֹהֵינוּ מֶלֶךְ הָעוֹלָם
הַזָּן אֶת־הָעוֹלָם כֻּלּוֹ בְּטוּבוֹ בְּחֵן בְּחֶסֶד וּבְרַחֲמִים.
הוּא נוֹתֵן לֶחֶם לְכָל־בָּשָׂר כִּי לְעוֹלָם חַסְדּוֹ.

וּבְטוּבוֹ הַגָּדוֹל תָּמִיד לֹא־חָסַר לָנוּ וְאַל יֶחְסַר־לָנוּ מָזוֹן לְעוֹלָם וָעֶד
בַּעֲבוּר שְׁמוֹ הַגָּדוֹל,
כִּי הוּא זָן וּמְפַרְנֵס לַכֹּל וּמֵטִיב לַכֹּל וּמֵכִין מָזוֹן לְכָל־בְּרִיּוֹתָיו
אֲשֶׁר בָּרָא.

בָּרוּךְ אַתָּה יְיָ
הַזָּן אֶת־הַכֹּל.

Creator of Many Souls

Blessed art thou, O Lord

our God, King of the universe,

Creator of many souls, and of their wants,

for all things thou hast created

to sustain each living soul.

Blessed be the Life of the universe.

בָּרוּךְ אַתָּה יְיָ

אֱלֹהֵינוּ מֶלֶךְ הָעוֹלָם

בּוֹרֵא נְפָשׁוֹת רַבּוֹת וְחֶסְרוֹנָן

עַל כָּל מַה שֶּׁבָּרָאתָ

לְהַחֲיוֹת בָּהֶם נֶפֶשׁ כָּל חָי.

בָּרוּךְ חֵי הָעוֹלָמִים.

After Deliverance from Danger

Benediction:

Blessed art thou, O Lord

our God, King of the universe,

who doest good to the undeserving,

and hast done all good to me.

Response:

He who hath done all good unto thee,

may He do all good unto thee forever.

ברכת הגומל

בָּרוּךְ אַתָּה יְיָ
אֱלֹהֵינוּ מֶלֶךְ הָעוֹלָם
הַגּוֹמֵל לְחַיָּבִים טוֹבוֹת
שֶׁגְּמָלַנִי כָּל־טוֹב.

מִי שֶׁגְּמָלְךָ כָּל־טוֹב
הוּא יִגְמָלְךָ כָּל־טוֹב סֶלָה.

My Father Art Thou

I will praise thee, O God of my salvation,

I will thank thee, O God of my father.

I will declare thy name, strength of my life,

for thou hast redeemed my soul from death.

Thou hast preserved my body from destruction

and from the power of Sheol thou didst deliver my soul....

My soul drew nigh unto death,

and my life to the nethermost Sheol.

And I turned about on every side and there was no man to

    help me,

I looked for one to uphold, but there was none.

Then thought I upon the compassion of the Lord,

and upon His mercies of old,

who delivereth them that wait for Him

and redeemeth them from all evil.

Then lifted I up my voice from the earth,

and cried out from the gates of Sheol.

Yea, I cried: "O Lord, my Father art thou,

for thou art the hero of my salvation;

leave me not in the days of my trouble,

in the day of wasteness and desolation.

I will praise thy name continually,

and will sing thy praise in prayer."

אֲהַלֶּלְךָ אֱלֹהֵי יִשְׁעִי

אוֹדְךָ אֱלֹהֵי אָבִי.

אֲסַפְּרָה שִׁמְךָ מָעוֹז חַיָּי

כִּי פָדִיתָ מִמָּוֶת נַפְשִׁי.

חָשַׂכְתָּ בְּשָׂרִי מִשָּׁחַת

וּמִיַּד שְׁאוֹל הִצַּלְתָּ נַפְשִׁי.

וַתִּגַּע לַמָּוֶת נַפְשִׁי

וְחַיָּתִי לִשְׁאוֹל תַּחְתִּיּוֹת.

וָאֶפְנֶה סָבִיב וְאֵין עוֹזֵר לִי

וָאֲצַפֶּה סוֹמֵךְ וָאָיִן.

וָאֶזְכְּרָה אֶת רַחֲמֵי יְיָ

וַחֲסָדָיו אֲשֶׁר מֵעוֹלָם.

הַמַּצִּיל אֶת חוֹסֵי בוֹ

וַיִּגְאָלֵם מִכָּל רָע.

וָאָרִים מֵאֶרֶץ קוֹלִי

וּמִשַּׁעֲרֵי שְׁאוֹל שִׁוַּעְתִּי.

וָאֲרוֹמֵם יְיָ אָבִי אַתָּה

כִּי אַתָּה גִבּוֹר יִשְׁעִי.

אַל תִּרְפֵּנִי בְּיוֹם צָרָה

בְּיוֹם שׁוֹאָה וּמְשׁוֹאָה.

אֲהַלְלָה שִׁמְךָ תָּמִיד

אֶזְכָּרְךָ בִּתְפִלָּה.

Wise in Thy Truth

I give [thanks unto thee, O Lord,] for thou hast given me insight into thy truth

and knowledge of thy wondrous secrets.

In loving-kindness to [lowly] man,

in abundance of mercy to wayward hearts,

who is like thee among the gods, O Lord,

and what truth is like thine?

Who can prove righteous in thy sight when thou bringest him
   unto judgment?

Not even a spirit can answer thy charge,

and none can withstand thy wrath.

Yet, all that are children of thy truth thou bringest before thee
   with forgiveness,

cleansing them of their transgressions

through thine abundant goodness, and through thy plenteous
   mercies,

causing them to stand in thy presence forever.

השכלתני באמתך

אוֹנְדְכָה אֲדוֹנָי! כִּי הִשְׂכַּלְתַּנִי בַּאֲמִתָּכָה

וּבְרָזֵי פִלְאֲכָה הוֹדַעְתַּנִי

וּבַחֲסָדֵיכָה לְאִישׁ נִתֹּהוּ!

בְּרוֹב רַחֲמֶיכָה לְנַעֲוֵי לֵב.

מִי כָמוֹכָה בָּאֵלִים אֲדוֹנָי

וּמִי כַאֲמִתֶּכָה

וּמִי יִצְנַד!זק לְפָנֶיכָה בְּהִשָׁפְטוֹ.

וְאֵין לְהָשִׁיב עַל תּוֹכַחְתָּכָה כּוֹל רוּחַ

וְלֹא יוּכַל כּוֹל לְהִתְיַצֵּב לִפְנֵי חֲמָתֶכָה.

וְכוֹל בְּנֵי אֲמִתֶּכָה תָּבִיא בִסְלִיחוֹת לְפָנֶיכָה

לְטַהֲרֵם מִפִּשְׁעֵיהֶם

בְּרוֹב טוּבְכָה וּבַהֲמוֹן רַנחַז!מֶיכָה

לְהַעֲמִידָם לְפָנֶיכָה לְעוֹלְמֵי עַד.

Streams in Dry Ground

I thank thee, O Lord, because thou hast put me

at a source of flowing streams in dry ground,

a spring of water in a land of drought,

channels watering a garden of delight,

a place of cedar and acacia,

together with pine for thy glory,

trees of life in a fount of mystery,

hidden amid all trees that drink water.

They shall put forth a branch for an eternal planting,

taking root before they sprout.

They shall send out their roots to the stream;

its stump shall be exposed to the living water;

and it shall become an eternal source.

מקור נוזלים ביבשה

אוֹנִדְךָה אֲדוֹנָי כִּי נְזַתַּתַּנִי
בִּמְקוֹר נוֹזְלִים בַּיַּבָּשָׁה
וּמַבּוּעַ מַיִם בְּאֶרֶץ צִיָּה
וּנמַזִשְׁקֵי גַן נ ... נָטַעְתָּזה
מַטַּע בְּרוֹשׁ וְתִדְהָר
עִם תְּאַשּׁוּר יַחַד לִכְבוֹדְךָה
עֲצֵי חַיִּים בְּמַעְיָן רָז
מְחוּבָּאִים בְּתוֹךְ כּוֹל עֲצֵי מָיִם.
וְהָיוּ לְהַפְרִיחַ נֵצֶר לְמַטַּעַת עוֹלָם
לְהַשְׁרִישׁ טֶרֶם יַפְרִיחוּ
וְשׁוֹרְשֵׁיהֶם לְיוּבָנלז יְשַׁלֵּחוּ
וְיִפָּתַח לְמַיִם חַיִּים וְגִזְעוֹ
וִיהִי לִמְקוֹר עוֹלָם.

Well I Know

Well I know, O Lord,

I was nought, and thou made me.

Thou formed and founded me,

"bestowed upon me life and mercy,

and didst with thy command my spirit guard."

Thou hast allowed me reason, wisdom, and insight;

girded me with the strength of thy power;

dowered me with thy wealth and honor,

and exalted me from height to height,

until, from day to day advancing,

thou hast brought me to this hour,

and to attain this present end.

יָדַעְתִּי יְיָ
כִּי לֹא הָיִיתִי וְאַתָּה עֲשִׂיתָנִי
אַתָּה יְצַרְתַּנִי וְכוֹנַנְתָּנִי
חַיִּים וָחֶסֶד עָשִׂיתָ עִמָּדִי
וּפְקֻדָּתְךָ שָׁמְרָה רוּחִי.

חָכְמָה וּתְבוּנָה הִשְׂכַּלְתָּנִי
וּמִכֹּחַ גְּבוּרָתְךָ אֲזַרְתָּנִי
וּמִן הָעֹשֶׁר וְהַכָּבוֹד אֲשֶׁר לְפָנֶיךָ הֶעֱנַקְתָּנִי
וּמִמַּעֲלָה לְמַעֲלָה רוֹמַמְתָּנִי
כְּמוֹ מִיָּמִים עַד יָמִים תַּשְׁלִימֵנִי
עַד אֲשֶׁר הֲבִיאוֹתַנִי עַד הֲלוֹם
וְהִגַּעְתַּנִי עַד הַקֵּץ הַזֶּה.

Father of Life

My Father, Father of orphans,

be gracious unto me,

send me the sun's rays as a gift.

And I, an orphan of orphans,

shall receive thy gift with thanks, with love, with hope.

I know how to prize thy gift, thy goodness, Selah!

My heart sings and shouts to thee,

O Father of life,

blessed art thou, Selah.

אָבִי, אֲבִי הַיְתוֹמִים

הֵיטֵב לִי

קַרְנֵי שֶׁמֶשׁ שָׁלַח לִי שַׁי.

וַאֲנִי יְתוֹם־הַיְתוֹמִים

אֲקַבֵּל מִנְחָתְךָ בְּתוֹדָה בְּאַהֲבָה בְּתִקְוָה.

אֲנִי יוֹדֵעַ לְהוֹקִיר אֶת מִנְחָתְךָ אֶת טוּבְךָ סֶלָה.

לִבִּי יְרַנֵּן אֵלֶיךָ אַף יְרוֹעַע

אֲבִי־הַחַיִּים

תְּבֹרַךְ סֶלָה.

Blessing of Death

Praised be thou, O Lord,
Spirit of the universe,
who brought me across the [Yabok] bridge of life.
When the dim light of my own self
will sink and merge
within the light which illumines
the world and eternity,
I shall conclude the order of my days.

In this twilight glow of my life,
I stand before the dawn of my new sun
with tense consciousness,
a man about to die and to live,
who feels at one with the universe and eternity,
as in the ancient words:
"Hear, O Israel, the Lord our God
the Lord is One."
Praised be the God of life and death,
of light and love.

ברכת המות

ברוך אתה ה׳ אלהי
רוח העולם,
אשר העברתני דרך מעבר יבק של החיים,
והיה אורי הדל הפרטי
שוקע וצולל
בהאור המאיר
על פני כל היקום והנצח
חסלתי את סדר זיו.

בין השמשות של יקומי וחיי,
עומד אני בהמית רוחי
לפני זריחת שמשי הצדה והכרתי הכוללת
האדם ההולך למות ולחיות
מרגיש באחדותו ואחריותו עם היקום והנצחי
כאשר הרגיש בזה המשל הקדמוני
שמע ישראל ה׳ אלהינו
ה׳ אחד
ברוך אלהי החיים והמות,
הזיו והחסד.

KNOWLEDGE

With Thee Is Wisdom

O God of my fathers, and Lord of mercy,

who hast made all things with thy word,

and ordained man through thy wisdom,

that he should have dominion over the creatures which thou

    hast made,

and order the world according to holiness and righteousness,

and execute judgment with an upright heart:

Give me wisdom, that sitteth by thy throne;

and reject me not from among thy children.

With thee is wisdom, which knoweth thy works,

and was present when thou madest the world,

and knew what was acceptable in thy sight,

and right in thy commandments.

O send her out of thy holy heavens,

and from the throne of thy glory bid her come,

that being present she may labor with me,

that I may know what is pleasing unto thee.

Who hath known thy counsel except thou give wisdom,

and send thy Holy Spirit from above?

For so the ways of them which lived on the earth were re-

    formed,

and men were taught the things that are pleasing unto thee,

and were saved through wisdom.

עִמְּךָ הַחָכְמָה

אֱלֹהֵי אֲבוֹתֵינוּ וַאֲדוֹן הָרַחֲמִים
אֲשֶׁר עָשִׂיתָ הַכֹּל בִּדְבָרֶךָ
וּבְחָכְמָתְךָ כּוֹנַנְתָּ אֱנוֹשׁ
לִמְשֹׁל בַּיְצוּרִים אֲשֶׁר בָּרָאתָ
לְכַלְכֵּל תֵּבֵל בְּקָדְשָׁהּ וּבְצֶדֶק
וּלְהוֹצִיא מִשְׁפָּט בְּיִשְׁרַת נָפֶשׁ.
תֶּן־לִי חָכְמָה הַיּוֹשֶׁבֶת עַל־יַד כִּסְאֶךָ
וְאַל תְּגָרְשֵׁנִי מִקֶּרֶב בָּנֶיךָ.

עִמְּךָ הַחָכְמָה הַיּוֹדַעַת מַעֲשֶׂיךָ
כִּי נֶעמְּךָ‫]‬הָיְתָה בְּבָרְאֲךָ אֶת־הָעוֹלָם
וְתֵדַע אֶת־הַיָּשָׁר בְּעֵינֶיךָ
וְאֶת הַטּוֹב לְפִי מִצְוֹתֶיךָ.
שְׁלַח אוֹתָהּ מִשְּׁמֵי קָדְשֶׁךָ
וּמִפְּנֵי כִסֵּא כְּבוֹדְךָ תִּפְקְדֶנָּה
לְמַעַן תִּשְׁכֹּן עִמִּי בַּעֲמָלִי
וְאֵדַע אֶת־הַיָּשָׁר לְפָנֶיךָ.

מִי הֵבִין עֲצָתְךָ בְּמָנְעֲךָ חָכְמָה
וְאֶת־רוּחַ קָדְשֶׁךָ לֹא תִשְׁלַח מִמְּרוֹמִים.
אַךְ אָז יֻכְּנוּ אָרְחוֹת]‬וְהָאֲנָשִׁים‫ [‬עֲלֵי־אֲדָמוֹת
וְיִלְמְדוּ בְּנֵי־אָדָם אֶת־הַיָּשָׁר לְפָנֶיךָ
וּבְחָכְמָה יִוָּשֵׁעוּ.

161

The Gift of Knowledge

Thou favorest the earthling with knowledge,
and teachest the mortal understanding,
favor us with knowledge,
wisdom and understanding from thee.

Blessed art thou, O Lord,
for the gift of knowledge.

דעת

אַתָּה חוֹנֵן לְאָדָם דַּעַת
וּמְלַמֵּד לֶאֱנוֹשׁ בִּינָה
חָנֵּנוּ מֵאִתְּךָ דֵּעָה
בִּינָה וְהַשְׂכֵּל.

בָּרוּךְ אַתָּה יְיָ
חוֹנֵן הַדָּעַת.

Our Father, the Father Compassionate

Our Father, the Father compassionate,

have compassion on us,

and put it in our heart

to understand and comprehend,

to hear, to learn, and to teach,

to watch, to do,

and to uphold all the words of instruction in thy Torah

with love.

Enlighten our eyes in thy Torah,

make our heart adhere to thy commandments,

unite our heart

to love and to revere thy name.

And let us never be shamed at all.

אָבִינוּ הָאָב הָרַחֲמָן הַמְרַחֵם
רַחֵם עָלֵינוּ
וְתֵן בְּלִבֵּנוּ
לְהָבִין וּלְהַשְׂכִּיל
לִשְׁמֹעַ לִלְמֹד וּלְלַמֵּד
לִשְׁמֹר וְלַעֲשׂוֹת
וּלְקַיֵּם אֶת כָּל דִּבְרֵי תַלְמוּד תּוֹרָתֶךָ
בְּאַהֲבָה.

וְהָאֵר עֵינֵינוּ בְּתוֹרָתֶךָ
וְדַבֵּק לִבֵּנוּ בְּמִצְוֹתֶיךָ
וְיַחֵד לְבָבֵנוּ
לְאַהֲבָה וּלְיִרְאָה אֶת שְׁמֶךָ
וְלֹא נֵבוֹשׁ לְעוֹלָם וָעֶד.

Thou Hast Taught Us Knowledge

Blessed art thou, O my God,

Who hast opened the heart of thy servant unto knowledge.

Direct all his works in righteousness,

and vouchsafe unto the son of thine handmaid

the favor which thou hast assured to all the mortal elect,

to stand in thy presence for ever.

For apart from thee no man's way can be perfect,

and without thy will is nothing wrought.

Thou it is that hath taught all knowledge,

and all things exist by thy will;

and there is none beside thee

to controvert thy plan;

none to understand all thy holy thought,

none to gaze into the depths of thy secrets,

none to perceive all thy wonders and the might of thy power.

Who can compass the sum of thy glory?

And what is mere mortal man amid thy wondrous works?

And what the child of woman to sit in thy presence?

בָּרוּךְ אַתָּה אֵלִי

הַפּוֹתֵחַ לְדֵעָה לֵב עַבְדְּכָה.

הָכֵן בְּצֶדֶק כּוֹל מַעֲשָׂיו

וְהָקֵם לְבֶן אֲמָתְכָה

כַּאֲשֶׁר רָצִיתָה לִבְחִירֵי אָדָם

לְהִתְיַצֵּב לְפָנֶיכָה לָעַד.

כִּיא מִבַּלְעָדֶיכָה לוֹא תִתֹּם דֶּרֶךְ

וּבְלִי רְצוֹנְכָה לוֹא יֵעָשֶׂה כּוֹל.

אַתָּה הוֹרֵיתָה כּוֹל דֵּעָה

וְכוֹל הַנִּהְיָה בִּרְצוֹנְכָה הָיָה.

וְאֵין אַחֵר זוּלָתֶכָה

לְהָשִׁיב עַל עֲצָתֶכָה

וּלְהַשְׂכִּיל בְּכוֹל מַחֲשֶׁבֶת קוֹדְשֶׁכָה.

וּלְהַבִּיט בְּעוֹמֶק רָזֶיכָה

וּלְהִתְבּוֹנֵן בְּכוֹל נִפְלָאוֹתֶיכָה עִם כּוֹחַ גְּבוּרָתֶכָה.

וּמִי יָכוֹל לְהָכִיל אֶת כְּבוֹדֶכָה.

וּמָה אַפֹּה הוּא בֶּן הָאָדָם בְּמַעֲשֵׂי פְלָאֶכָה.

וִילִיד אִשָּׁה מַה יֵּשֵׁב לְפָנֶיכָה.

That Thy Torah Be Our Craft

Be it thy will,

O Lord our God,

that thy Torah be our craft,

that our hearts be not overcast,

nor our eyes somber.

תהא תורתך אמנותנו

יְהִי רָצוֹן מִלְּפָנֶיךָ

יְיָ אֱלֹהֵינוּ

שֶׁתְּהֵא תוֹרָתְךָ אֻמָּנוּתֵנוּ

וְאַל יִדְוֶה לִבֵּנוּ

וְאַל יֶחְשְׁכוּ עֵינֵינוּ.

The Crown of Torah

My Father who art in heaven,

blessed be thy great name for all eternity

and mayest thou find contentment from Israel, thy servants,
wherever they may dwell.

Thou hast reared us, made us great, sanctified us, praised us;

thou hast bound on us the crown of the words of Torah,

they that reach from one end of the world to the other.

Whatever of Torah I have fulfilled, came only through thee;

whatever loving-kindness I have shown, came only through
thee;

in return for the little of Torah that I have done before thee

thou hast given me a share in this world, in the days of the
Messiah, and in the world to come.

כתר דברי תורה

אבי שבשמים
יהי שמך הגדול מבורך לעולם ולעולמי עולמים.
ותהא לך קורת רוח מישראל עבדיך בכל מקומות מושבותיהן
על שגידלתנו ורוממתנו וקידשתנו וקילסתנו
וקשרת לנו כתר דברי תורה מסוף העולם ועד סופו.
תורה שעשיתי לא עשיתי אלא משלך.
גמילות חסדים שעשיתי לא עשיתי אלא משלך.
ובשכר תורה קימעה שעשיתי לפניך
הקנית נלי[ז] העולם הזה וימות המשיח ועולם הבא.

THE CYCLE OF
LIFE

The Blessing after the Circumcision

Our God and God of our fathers,

preserve this child to his father and to his mother.

His name shall be called in Israel ... the son of ....

Let the father be glad with him that came forth from his loins,

and the mother rejoice in the fruit of her womb.

As it is written:

"Let thy father and thy mother be glad,

and let her that bore thee rejoice."

And it is said:

"And I passed thee, and I saw thee weltering in thy blood,

and I said unto thee in thy blood, 'live!'

Yea, I said unto thee in thy blood, 'live!'"

"Give thanks to the Lord, who is good,

who is gracious for ever."

This little child...,—may he grow into manhood.

Even as he has come into the covenant,

so may he come to Torah,

to the nuptial canopy,

and to good deeds.

קִים אֶת הַיֶּלֶד הַזֶּה

אֱלֹהֵינוּ וֵאלֹהֵי אֲבוֹתֵינוּ
קַיֵּם אֶת־הַיֶּלֶד הַזֶּה לְאָבִיו וּלְאִמּוֹ
וְיִקָּרֵא שְׁמוֹ בְּיִשְׂרָאֵל ‹פְּלוֹנִי בֶּן פְּלוֹנִי›.
יִשְׂמַח הָאָב בְּיוֹצֵא חֲלָצָיו
וְתָגֵל אִמּוֹ בִּפְרִי בִטְנָהּ.
כַּכָּתוּב

יִשְׂמַח אָבִיךָ וְאִמֶּךָ
וְתָגֵל יוֹלַדְתֶּךָ.
וְנֶאֱמַר

וָאֶעֱבֹר עָלַיִךְ וָאֶרְאֵךְ מִתְבּוֹסֶסֶת בְּדָמָיִךְ
וָאֹמַר לָךְ בְּדָמַיִךְ חֲיִי
וָאֹמַר לָךְ בְּדָמַיִךְ חֲיִי.
הוֹדוּ לַיְיָ כִּי־טוֹב
כִּי לְעוֹלָם חַסְדּוֹ.
זֶה הַקָּטוֹן ‹פְּלוֹנִי› גָּדוֹל יִהְיֶה
כְּשֵׁם שֶׁנִּכְנַס לַבְּרִית
כֵּן יִכָּנֵס לַתּוֹרָה
וּלְחֻפָּה
וּלְמַעֲשִׂים טוֹבִים.

Bridegroom and Bride

Blessed art thou, O Lord our God, King of the universe,

who hath created joy and gladness, bridegroom and bride,

mirth and exultation, pleasure and delight,

love and brotherhood, peace and friendship.

May there soon be heard in the cities of Judah, and in the
    streets of Jerusalem,

the voice of joy and gladness,

the voice of the bridegroom and the voice of the bride,

the jubilant voice of bridegrooms from the wedding canopy,

and of youths from their feasts of song.

Blessed art thou, O Lord,

who gives the bridegroom joy in his bride.

קוֹל חָתָן וְקוֹל כַּלָּה

בָּרוּךְ אַתָּה יְיָ אֱלֹהֵינוּ מֶלֶךְ הָעוֹלָם
אֲשֶׁר בָּרָא שָׂשׂוֹן וְשִׂמְחָה חָתָן וְכַלָּה
גִּילָה רִנָּה דִּיצָה וְחֶדְוָה
אַהֲבָה וְאַחֲוָה וְשָׁלוֹם וְרֵעוּת.
מְהֵרָה יְיָ אֱלֹהֵינוּ יִשָּׁמַע בְּעָרֵי יְהוּדָה וּבְחוּצוֹת יְרוּשָׁלַיִם
קוֹל שָׂשׂוֹן וְקוֹל שִׂמְחָה
קוֹל חָתָן וְקוֹל כַּלָּה
קוֹל מִצְהֲלוֹת חֲתָנִים מֵחֻפָּתָם
וּנְעָרִים מִמִּשְׁתֵּה נְגִינָתָם.
בָּרוּךְ אַתָּה יְיָ
מְשַׂמֵּחַ חָתָן עִם הַכַּלָּה.

Grant Them Mercy

Blessed art thou, O God, with all pure blessing;

let them bless thee for ever.

And blessed art thou, because thou hast made me joyful;

and that hath not come to me which I suspected,

but thou hast dealt with us according to thy great mercy.

And blessed art thou,

because thou hast had mercy on two that are the only-begotten

    children of their parents;

grant them mercy, O Lord,

and fulfil their life with joy and mercy.

עשה עמהם רחמים

בָּרוּךְ אַתָּה אֱלֹהִים בְּכָל בְּרָכָה טְהוֹרָה
יְבָרְכוּךְ עַד־כָּל הַדּוֹרוֹת.
וּבָרוּךְ אַתָּה כִּי שִׂמַּחְתַּנִי
וְלֹא הָיָה כַּאֲשֶׁר חָשַׁבְתִּי
כִּי אִם־בְּרַחֲמֶיךָ הָרַבִּים עָשִׂיתָ עִמָּנוּ.
וּבָרוּךְ אַתָּה
כִּי רִחַמְתָּ עַל־שְׁנֵי הַיְלָדִים הַיְחִידִים
עֲשֵׂה עִמָּהֶם אֲדֹנָי רַחֲמִים
וּמַלֵּא אֶת־חַיֵּיהֶם שִׂמְחָה וְרַחֲמִים.

Into Thine Hand

Blessed be the Lord by day.

Blessed be the Lord by night.

Blessed be the Lord when we lie down.

Blessed be the Lord when we rise up.

For in thine hand are the souls of the living and the dead

—"in whose hand is the soul of every living thing

and the breath of all flesh."

Into thine hand I entrust my spirit:

thou hast redeemed me, O Lord, God of truth.

Our God who art in heaven,

reveal unto us thy oneness

and establish thy kingdom

and reign over us

forever.

בידך אפקיד רוחי

בָּרוּךְ יְיָ בַּיּוֹם

בָּרוּךְ יְיָ בַּלַּיְלָה

בָּרוּךְ יְיָ בְּשָׁכְבֵנוּ

בָּרוּךְ יְיָ בְּקוּמֵנוּ.

כִּי בְיָדְךָ נַפְשׁוֹת הַחַיִּים וְהַמֵּתִים.

אֲשֶׁר בְּיָדוֹ נֶפֶשׁ כָּל חָי

וְרוּחַ כָּל בְּשַׂר־אִישׁ.

בְּיָדְךָ אַפְקִיד רוּחִי

פָּדִיתָה אוֹתִי יְיָ אֵל אֱמֶת.

אֱלֹהֵינוּ שֶׁבַּשָּׁמַיִם

יַחֵד שְׁמָךְ

וְקַיֵּם מַלְכוּתְךָ תָּמִיד

וּמְלוֹךְ עָלֵינוּ

לְעוֹלָם וָעֶד.

Who Drops the Bonds of Sleep

Blessed art thou, O Lord
our God, King of the universe,
who drops the bonds of sleep on my eyes,
and slumber on my eyelids;
who enlightens the pupil of the eye.

Be it thy will,
O Lord my God and God of my fathers,
to lay me down in peace,
and to raise me again to life and peace.

May the Will-to-Good control me,
and not the Will-to-Evil;
save me from the Will-to-Evil,
and from grave illnesses;
may no dream of evil scare me,
nor any evil contemplations.

Perfect be my bed before thee,
and my eyes enlighten, lest I sleep on into death.

Blessed art thou, O Lord,
who enlightens all the universe
with his glory.

המפיל חבלי שנה

בָּרוּךְ אַתָּה יְיָ
אֱלֹהֵינוּ מֶלֶךְ הָעוֹלָם
הַמַּפִּיל חֶבְלֵי שֵׁנָה עַל עֵינַי
וּתְנוּמָה עַל עַפְעַפָּי
וּמֵאִיר לְאִישׁוֹן בַּת עָיִן.

יְהִי רָצוֹן מִלְפָנֶיךָ
יְיָ אֱלֹהַי וֵאלֹהֵי אֲבוֹתַי
שֶׁתַּשְׁכִּיבֵנִי לְשָׁלוֹם
וְתַעֲמִידֵנִי לְחַיִּים וּלְשָׁלוֹם.

וְיִשְׁלוֹט בִּי יֵצֶר הַטוֹב
וְאַל יִשְׁלוֹט בִּי יֵצֶר הָרָע
וְתַצִּילֵנִי מִיֵּצֶר הָרָע
וּמֵחֳלָיִם רָעִים
וְאַל יְבַהֲלוּנִי חֲלוֹמוֹת
וְהִרְהוּרִים רָעִים.

וּתְהִי מִטָּתִי שְׁלֵמָה לְפָנֶיךָ
וְהָאֵר עֵינַי פֶּן אִישַׁן הַמָּוֶת.

בָּרוּךְ אַתָּה יְיָ
הַמֵּאִיר לָעוֹלָם כֻּלּוֹ
בִּכְבוֹדוֹ.

Bless Thou... This Year

Bless thou, O Lord our God,
this year
and all its varieties of harvest
for our good.

And lay thou a blessing
upon the face of the earth,

sate us with thy bounty,
and bless our year
like the goodly years.

Blessed art thou, O Lord,
who blesses the years.

בָּרֵךְ עָלֵינוּ יְיָ אֱלֹהֵינוּ
אֶת הַשָּׁנָה הַזֹּאת
וְאֶת כָּל מִינֵי תְבוּאָתָהּ
לְטוֹבָה

וְתֵן בְּרָכָה
עַל פְּנֵי הָאֲדָמָה

וְשַׂבְּעֵנוּ מִטּוּבֶךָ
וּבָרֵךְ שְׁנָתֵנוּ
כַּשָּׁנִים הַטּוֹבוֹת.

בָּרוּךְ אַתָּה יְיָ
מְבָרֵךְ הַשָּׁנִים.

Thou Givest All, Taking Nought

...sanctify, sustain, gather, govern, establish, glorify,

confirm, pasture, raise up, enlighten, pacify, administer, per⁄

    fect—

the people which thou hast established,

the peculiar people, the people which thou hast ransomed,

the people which thou hast called, thy people, the sheep of thy

    pasture.

Thou art the only physician of our ailing souls,

keep us in thy joy,

heal us in sickness,

cast us not away as unfit to receive thy healing.

The word of thy mouth is the giver of health.

These things we beg of thee, Master:

remit whatever we have done amiss,

check whatever leads us to sin,

neither record against us all that we have done unlawfully.

Forgiveness of sin is the expression of thy long⁄suffering.

It is a fair thing, O Immortal, not to be wroth with mortals,

doomed to destruction, short⁄lived, inhabiting a toilsome world.

Never dost thou cease to do good, for thou art bountiful;

thou givest all, taking nought, for thou lackest nothing;

᾽ΑΓΙΑΣΟΝ

ἁγίασον, διάθρεψον, ἐπισύναξον, διοίκησον

στήρισον, δόξασον, βεβαίωσον, ποίμανον,

ἀνάστησον, φώτ[ισ]ον, εἰρήνευσον, οἰκο

νόμησον, τελίωσον)――― τ[ὸν λαὸ]ν

ὃν ἐκτίσω, τὸν λαὸν τὸν [π]εριούσιον,

τὸν λαὸν ὅν ἐλ[υ]τρώσω, [τ]ὸν λαὸν ὃν

ἐκάλεσας, τὸν λαόν σου, [τὰ] πρόβατα τῆς

νομῆς σου. [ψ]υχῆς ἡμῶν ν[ο]σούσης ἰατρὸς

μόνος εἶ σύ, σῇ ἀγαλλ[ιάσει . .]ρει, νοσέοντας

ἡμᾶς θεράπευσον, μὴ ἡμᾶς ἀπ[ο]ρίψῃς

ὡς ἀδέκτ[ο]υς σῆς θεραπ[εί]ας. σοῦ ἀπὸ

στόματος λόγ.[ο]s ὑγιείας [ἐ]στὶν δοτήρ.

ταῦτ' αἰτούμεθα παρ[ὰ σοῦ,] δέσποτα, παρὲς

ὅσα ἡμάρτομεν, κάτ[εχε] εἴ τι ἀμαρτάνειν

[φ]έρι, καὶ μὴ [ἡ]μῶν κ[ατα]γράψῃς ὅσα πα-

ρανόμως ἐπράξαμεν. [σ]ῆς ἀνεξικακίας

ἔργον ἄφεσις ἁμαρτιῶν. εὐπρεπον ἐστιν,

ἄφθιτε, θνητοῖς μὴ κιτέειν ἐπικηρίοις,

ὀλιγοβίοις, ἐπίμοχθον [γ]ῆν ἔχουσιν. εὐ-

[ερ]γετῶν οὐ διαλείπεις, ἄφθονος γὰρ εἶ σύ,

πᾶν δίδως, οὐθὲν λαμβάνων, ἀνεν-

δεὴς γὰρ εἶ, πᾶν ἀγαθόν [ἐσ]τιν σόν, κακὸν

every righteous thing is thine, unrighteousness alone is not
thine.

Evil is that which thou wouldst not, the child of our imagi-
nations.—

Receive from us these psalmodies, these hymnodies, these
prayers,

these supplications, these entreaties, these requests,

these confessions, these petitions, these thanksgivings,

this readiness, this earnestness, these vigils, these...,

these couchings upon the earth, these prayerful utterances.

Having a kindly master in thee, the eternal King,

we beseech thee to behold our pitiful state....

δὲ μόνον οὐ σόν, φαῦλόν ἐστιν ὅ μὴ
θέλεις, τέκος ἐννοιῶν ἡμετερῶν)————
προσδέξαι παρ' ἡμῶν τὰς ψαλμῳδίας,
τὰς ὑμνῳδίας, τὰς εὐχάς, τὰς παρακλή-
σεις, τὰς δεήσεις, τὰς ἀξιώσεις, τὰς
ἐξομολογήσεις, τὰς αἰτήσεις, τὰς εὐχαριστίας,
τὴν προθυμίαν, τὴν σπουδήν, τὰς ἀγρυπνί-
ας, τὰς . . . . [. .]είας, τὰς χαμευνίας, τὰς
εὐκτηρίους φωνάς. φιλάνθρωπον ἔχ[ον-]
τες δεσπότην, σὲ τὸν αἰώνιων βασιλέα,
ἱκετεύομεν τὰ καθ' ἡμᾶς οἴκτου ἄξια

Who Formed You in Judgment

Blessed art thou, O Lord our God, King of the universe,

who formed you in judgment,

who nourished and sustained you in judgment,

who brought death on you in judgment,

who knows the number of you all,

and will hereafter restore you to life in judgment.

Blessed art thou, O Lord,

who quickens the dead.

אשר יצר אתכם בדין

בָּרוּךְ אַתָּה יְיָ אֱלֹהֵינוּ מֶלֶךְ הָעוֹלָם
אֲשֶׁר־יָצַר אֶתְכֶם בַּדִּין
וְזָן וְכִלְכֵּל אֶתְכֶם בַּדִּין
וְהֵמִית אֶתְכֶם בַּדִּין
וְיוֹדֵעַ מִסְפַּר כֻּלְּכֶם
וְעָתִיד לְהַחֲזִיר וּלְהַחֲיוֹתְכֶם בַּדִּין.

בָּרוּךְ אַתָּה יְיָ
מְחַיֶּה הַמֵּתִים.

Kaddish

Mighty, hallowed ever be His great name

in the world He has created according to His will.

May He establish His kingdom

in the days of your life

and in the life of the whole house of Israel

speedily.

Let us say, Amen.

May His great name be blessed unto all eternity.

Blessed and praised, honored, adored and extolled,

glorified and exalted,

be the name of the Holy One, blessed be He.

He is high above all blessings and hymns, praises

and words of solace which are uttered throughout the world.

Let us say, Amen.

May there be abundant peace from heaven,

and life for us and for all Israel.

Let us say, Amen.

May He who makes peace on high

bring peace to us and to all Israel.

Let us say, Amen.

Do you usually blame yourself? This is the time in therapy to accept that no amount of work on yourself will change certain impossible situations. It may be time to let go of and mourn the disappointing reality. (See page 120 for a discussion of this subject.)

• *Flight from separation.*   Do you hate to say goodbye? Have you noticed a problem with separating in other situations?

If you are aware that you have gotten what you came for and that very little new is happening in your therapy, you may be avoiding separation. If separation is an issue for you, a carefully planned termination can provide the time and space for you to resolve separation issues.

• *Fear of disapproval.*   A corollary of the flight from separation is staying in therapy to avoid real or imagined disapproval. You may feel grateful to your therapist or loyal to the members of your group and believe that it would be hurtful to leave them.

I might stay in therapy longer than I need because

After some discussion, you may decide that your therapist's assessment makes sense and that this is a good time to leave. On the other hand, your therapist may decide that you have more to gain and will continue your therapy or refer you to another therapist. For a number of clients, therapy provides a needed resource unavailable in their families or their communities, and, by necessity, the course of their treatment may cover a great many years. Many therapists recognize this and are willing to continue working with clients who need long-term therapy. If your therapist practices in a way that precludes this possibility and you think that you need to continue your therapy, speak with your current therapist about transferring to a therapist who can see you for a longer period of time.

◆

"I had a very difficult childhood. I do have a good job, friends, a stable life, yet I am always frightened and suspicious. I need to keep checking out my thinking with someone outside the situation

in order to figure out what's going on. Some people don't understand my being in therapy for so many years, but I know that I really need it."

◆

When Other Issues Cloud Your Therapist's Judgment

Occasionally therapists who have been caring and consistent become transformed into insistent, even angry people when the subject of termination is raised. Separation provokes complex feelings for everyone, including therapists. Your therapist may have professional or personal reasons for encouraging you to stay or leave.

Other issues may cloud a therapist's judgment. The financial or personal loss when a client leaves may play a part. A therapist may be reluctant to give up a gratifying relationship with a client.

Although you could gain more from therapy, your therapist may for his or her own reasons suggest that you end your therapy. He or she may feel inadequate to address your issues or may be unable to overcome countertransference reactions (see page 157). He may be cutting back on his practice or be preoccupied with problems. Or your therapist may just be mistaken in his or her assessment of your readiness to end now.

If, after discussion, you and your therapist don't agree, you can seek a second opinion to help you decide how to proceed. (For information about obtaining a consultation, turn to page 166.)

NOTE: It can be difficult for a therapist to let you go if you are still in pain. It can be especially hard to let you end therapy if you are still self-destructive, if you are damaging someone else, or if you experience one or more of the serious symptoms on page 22. In these instances, it is not time for you to leave therapy.

I imagine my therapist's issues about my leaving are

When we discussed my fantasy, I learned

These are the questions that I still have for my therapist

◆

"I kept telling him that I wanted more. Sure I'm a better parent and my career is going well, but I still feel bad about myself. After his trying to show me that I was finished with therapy and my trying to tell him I needed more, he decided to refer me to another therapist, who could help me."

"When I decided to leave my therapeutic community, my therapist told me that there was no hope for me to change unless I stayed with them. I left. At first it was hard for me to hold on to my own strengths. It was the right decision. If I stayed like my boyfriend did, I would be dependent on them forever."

"My therapist was scared of my husband's temper. He made nice to him and told us we were doing well enough to stop therapy. I felt cheated."

◆

Consider Other Opinions

Your therapist may not be the only one with an opinion about your readiness to leave therapy. Other important people may have strong views about your ending therapy. Is anyone encouraging you to leave therapy before you are ready or to stay in therapy longer than seems necessary?

Sometimes family, lovers, or friends are uncomfortable with our being in therapy. Many times parents or partners are frightened that they will be blamed by therapists or be criticized by us and lose our love. They may worry that something is seriously wrong and want reassurance that all is well. Once the therapy ends, they will be relieved of their fear or worry.

Other times, people may have goals for us that we don't share. Did you begin therapy because someone else was concerned about you or bothered by some aspect of your behavior? Is there someone in your life now who wants you to be different from the way you are?

Evaluating other people's feedback is a good idea. Often there may be something you can learn. If someone in your life has an opinion about whether you ought to stay in or leave therapy, use the next exercises to consider his or her thinking. In the process, ask yourself if you have been talking with them about your therapy in a way that would encourage them to over- or undervalue it.

_____ (insert name) recommends that I (stay in) (leave) (change to) another therapy because

My therapist thinks I (ought to consider) (can proceed in spite of) this recommendation because

◆

"I am so self-destructive at times that the only reason I stay in therapy, or stay alive, for that matter, is because I know my therapist and my group really care about me. Even though I am staying for them, I suppose I'm really staying for myself."

"I've been in therapy for a year now, and I still don't think my being turned on to kids, fondling them and having them touch me is so bad. It's not like I'm having intercourse with them. The only reason that I go to therapy is that my wife will leave me if I don't."

"My husband wants me to stay in therapy so I will be more 'cooperative' with him. That sounds reasonable, except what he means by cooperative is really submissive. He can't stand how I've learned to be myself since therapy has begun."

◆ Task 3 ◆
Make a Decision

Having thought through why you want to leave and what more you might get from continuing, you may feel better equipped to make your decision. You can take your therapist's opinion and the desires of other people into account, but under most circumstances, it is up to you to make the decision for yourself.

Keep in mind that deciding to leave does not mean that you end immediately. Following your decision, you will begin the termination phase of your therapy, during which you will have the chance to say a thoughtful goodbye. The next chapter will guide you in this process.

When External Circumstances Dictate Your Ending

In some cases, the decision to end therapy is not yours to make. You may be going to a clinic where the total number of sessions is limited or where therapists leave their jobs or complete their training and move on. Something in your or your therapist's life may interfere with the continuation of your therapy.

◆

"My therapist told me that he was leaving the clinic, and that if I wanted to I could be 'transferred' to another therapist. I felt like an object being passed on to someone else."

"I got this great job in another city and had to leave therapy. But I just wasn't ready. My therapist worked out a way for me to see him once a month and have phone sessions until ending seems right."

"I will miss my group; after four years they are like a family to me. I love and trust my therapist; if only she weren't moving and disbanding the group. I've been crying for months. She says that I can go to marathon group sessions after she's moved, but it will never be the same."

◆

Your therapist may ask you to leave because you are breaking important rules. Usually your therapist will have suggestions about where you can go to get further assistance.

◆

"I was an undergraduate and I was broke all the time. The counseling center only charged five dollars a session, but I never had it. The counselor said that I didn't seem to care enough about therapy to make it a priority and to come back when I was ready to work."

"We could not be high and come to group. When I continued to drink right before sessions, the therapist told me I couldn't come back again and gave me the name of a good alcoholism program."

◆

What Have You Decided?

Review what you have learned, and then answer the following questions.

It is better for me to continue my therapy now because

I am going to take a break from my therapy because

I am ready to begin the process of leaving therapy now because

I am going to continue discussing ending my therapy because

Take the Time for an Ending Phase of Therapy

Whatever you have decided, you have just gone through a very important process of self-exploration. If you are staying in therapy, turn back to Chapters 7 and 8 and continue your journey. If you have decided to leave, you will be embarking on the final phase of your therapy. Even if the decision to end your therapy has been marked by conflict with your therapist or is beyond your control, it is worthwhile to go through as much of a termination process as circumstances permit. You have a lot to gain by a carefully considered leave-taking. Be sure to read the next chapter before you actually end your therapy.

·11·
Leaving Therapy

TASKS

1. Explore Your Reactions to Ending Therapy
2. Plan Your Leave-Taking
3. Complete Your Therapy
4. Say Goodbye

Now that you have decided to end therapy, an important part of your work lies ahead—the actual leave-taking. This final phase of your therapy is just as important as the beginning and middle phases; a thoughtful, fully experienced ending will protect and extend all the work you've done so far.

A great deal may happen between your decision to end and the last session. Like preparing to leave home, you need time to get used to the idea of leaving a safe and familiar place that holds personal history and meaning. You will have a chance to pack what you want to take along, plan for your new life, tie up all the loose ends, reminisce, and say goodbye. This chapter guides you through all of this.

◆ Task 1 ◆
Explore Your Reactions to Ending Therapy

Endings stir up complicated feelings in all of us. During the last phase of therapy, you are dealing with ending an important relationship and at the same time you may be struggling with the ghosts of past endings.

This ending can be painful, bittersweet, joyous, a great relief, or a combination of these feelings. To avoid dealing with these feelings you may be tempted to continue as usual. Sessions may go by without mentioning the upcoming ending. You or your therapist may be tempted to ignore, run away from, or rush through this final phase of therapy. Make your reactions a part of your therapy so that the process will be a rich one for you. Use this time for your benefit. Neither rush the ending nor prolong it.

The next exercise helps you be aware of what you feel as you end this experience. Check as many statements as apply and use the blank space to write about them if you like.

As I contemplate ending therapy I feel

_____ satisfied with my experience in therapy.
_____ relieved that I no longer have to go to sessions.
_____ disappointed that I haven't gotten more from therapy.
_____ proud of how far I've come.
_____ angry because I have to leave.
_____ sad to leave my therapist or group.
_____ excited about the future.
_____ impatient to see what it will be like without therapy.
_____ pleased that I will have more time and money for myself.
_____ scared that I will be abandoned or rejected by my therapist.
_____ overwhelmed, lost, or frightened at the thought of being without therapy.
_____ guilty about leaving.
_____ grateful for all I've gotten.
_____ very little of anything.
_____ or, _____

Your reactions will probably change as time goes on. You may want to return to this checklist from time to time to note and understand any changes in your feelings.

◆

"When I think about ending therapy I think about a kind of death. I think of how precious the relationship is and how I will miss it.

Then, I think of a kind of rebirth; living more freely emotionally, without the commitment or expense of therapy."

"We worry that without couples' therapy we'll be jinxed back into being unpleasant and bored with each other."

"When I first decided to end, I felt nostalgic and grateful to my therapist. Then even though it was my idea to stop therapy, I found myself feeling rejected and angry. Now I feel more balanced. I like Dr. R and respect the work we've done together."

◆

The way we leave therapy is often reminiscent of how we have reacted to other important partings. Just as you did in the beginning and middle phases, explore how you usually deal with endings. Anticipating what may happen will give you more control over what actually happens.

Here are some common styles of separating. Although at first glance they may appear to be different, they have some things in common. When we adopt any one of these patterns we are attempting to make the process of leave-taking easier by minimizing the discomfort of separating. Yet, by failing to acknowledge and deal with all of our reactions, we limit the richness of the experience. As you thought back to past endings you may have identified some patterns of your own. Have you ended relationships or experiences in one or another or a mixture of these styles?

Styles of Separating

♦ *Avoiding goodbyes.* Often we ignore the upcoming leave-taking in the hope that we will spare ourselves (and possibly others) uncomfortable or painful feelings. We may worry that others will not care whether or not we say goodbye. Or we may be expressing our disappointment in the experience by leaving without saying farewell. Not saying goodbye is also a way of denying that it is really over.

◆

"I didn't hug my favorite camp counselor goodbye or exchange addresses with the kids in my bunk. I didn't go to my high school

graduation or let my parents drive me to college. When my favorite aunt was dying, I didn't visit her in the hospital, and I didn't go to her funeral when she died. When I decided to end therapy, I was tempted to stop coming without much discussion."

◆

◆ ***Using anger to separate.***   You may find yourself more at home with anger than with the other emotions that leave-taking inspires. You may feel that the anger will protect you from other more painful emotions such as longing and sadness, or even joy. Sometimes we use anger to help us justify the fact that we are ending.

◆

"I had a fight with my best friend in third grade when she moved to the suburbs. I battled my parents when I was 18 and left home. I have been fired from jobs that I didn't like by getting the boss riled. I notice that I keep trying to pick a fight with my therapist and group now that I'm discussing leaving therapy."

◆

◆ ***Staying around for crumbs.***   Afraid that we may miss something important by leaving, or worried that we won't be able to manage alone, we stay in a relationship longer than necessary. Yet often we stay for minimal returns.

◆

"I stick around feeling cheated and angry; I can't leave until I get what I want. I have held onto the most impossible friends, hoping they would come through. Now I am refusing to set the date to leave, always wanting something more."

◆

◆ ***Devaluing the past.***   It can seem easier to leave something that wasn't any good in the first place than to leave something of value. When we devalue an experience or a relationship we can cushion painful feelings about leaving since we convince ourselves that there is nothing really to miss.

◆

"I am always glad to move on. I can't imagine why I hung around so long. I don't like to waste my time thinking about the past. I feel that I got nothing out of therapy, it was a great disappointment."

◆

• **Denying the importance of leaving.** We can protect ourselves from the complex feelings about leaving by minimizing the importance of leaving and not feeling much.

◆

"We moved around quite a bit when I was a kid and I don't think that separations are a problem for me. Ending therapy doesn't need to be a big deal."

◆

As I reflect on the way I've ended things in the past, I see that I

If I follow my usual pattern during the ending phase of therapy I may

I would like to end differently this time by

Doubts About Leaving Are Common

It is possible to be eager and move on and, at the same time, to want to hold onto what is familiar and safe. Having mixed feelings about leaving therapy is to be expected in this ending phase. Do you experience any of the following signs of ambivalence? Check those statements that apply.

_____ I wonder if I can make it on my own.
_____ I thought I had worked out a problem and now it is recurring.

_____ I am finding new issues to talk about as I am leaving.

_____ I am developing new symptoms since I have decided to end.

_____ I find that there is a part of me that wants to stay in this secure relationship.

If you have checked any of these statements, be assured. These are common occurrences in the final phase of therapy. Whenever we leave something of value we will have some second thoughts.

◆

"I keep dreaming that I am climbing a rickety ladder and the rungs won't hold me. I am in constant danger of falling. That's just what I fear will happen without therapy."

"I've always held a little part of me in reserve. In the beginning of therapy I thought that when I could let myself feel that my therapist was my best friend, I'd be ready to end therapy. Now I feel that way and I don't want to leave!"

"My lover and I started having the same old fights again just before our last sessions. When we recognized what was happening, we burst out laughing because we were so sure that we had no doubts about leaving."

◆ Task 2 ◆
Plan Your Leave-Taking

How long will you and your therapist take to conclude your therapy and say goodbye? The length of the final phase of your therapy will depend on your unique situation and your therapist's approach to therapy.

If you are in a short form of therapy, you may have been discussing termination from the beginning. If you are in a setting where the ending date is predetermined, you and your therapist will be involved in planning how to use your final sessions meaningfully rather than in deciding when to end.

If your therapy has been going on for more than a year, you may spend several months talking about leaving. If your therapy is longer term, a proportionately longer time will be spent on ending. You and your therapist need to discuss what is best for you.

How would you like to end therapy? Below are some different ending plans. Discuss your choice in therapy; your therapist may recommend that one or a combination of these is best for you.

- *A gradual ending.* You taper off, seeing your therapist less frequently than usual. You may cut down to once a week, once every two weeks, or monthly. You will have a taste of what ending therapy will be like.
- *An issue oriented ending.* You and your therapist decide that you will end therapy once you finish working on a particular theme or problem. Once the work is done you will leave therapy.
- *A specific date is set.* You and/or your therapist set the ending time. Barring emergencies, you will use the allotted time to complete any unfinished business.

◆ Task 3 ◆
Complete Your Therapy

As you move through the ending phase, a lot of unexpected emotional issues may arise. Your therapy may very well accelerate or intensify in this last phase and you may be surprised by the amount you accomplish.

Tie Up Loose Ends

Is there something you want to work on before you set the date for your last session? Have you left some issue for last?

Before leaving therapy, I want to

◆

"I have saved one problem for last. I smoke a joint every night before I go to bed. After I work that one out I'll be ready to stop therapy."

"Before we leave I want us to have a couple of fights and to resolve them without resorting to deafening silence for weeks on end."

"When my daughter gets another F and I don't get depressed and blame myself, I'll know that I'm cured. I can't believe that for once I'm actually looking forward to the possibility that she will mess up just to see how I'll handle it."

◆

Review Your Therapy with Your Therapist

One of the most meaningful parts of leave-taking can be reviewing your therapy with your therapist. It gives each of you a chance to share your perspective on the work you have done.

You may find that your therapist is more forthcoming than usual. Even therapists whose style is fairly neutral may become more personal as the end of therapy approaches.

As you respond to the next statements think about what you would like to share with your therapist.

What I appreciate about my therapy with you is

I've always wanted you to know

Remember when

I wish that I

I wish that you

I would like to ask you

If others are involved in therapy with you, go through these exercises again this time keeping your partner, group, or family members in mind.

Allow Yourself to Mourn

Many of us experience a sense of loss as we face the end of therapy. You may feel mournful about leaving behind the important relationship with your therapist and the unique experience of therapy. It can be surprising to discover that you are also mourning other less expected losses. You may miss the parts of yourself that you have changed as a result of therapy as well as the unrealistic expectations for a more perfect you.

YOUR THERAPY

You may feel relieved that you no longer need therapy, yet you may also anticipate its absence as a loss.

I will miss
_____ a special time to think and talk about myself.
_____ having a place to problem solve.
_____ working with someone on my behalf.
_____ the opportunity to gain insight and awareness.
_____ the encouragement to express my feelings.
_____ knowing that someone understands.

_____ having a place to explore fantasies, dreams, and my unconscious life.

_____ getting ideas about how to handle things.

_____ the closeness between me and my therapist or group.

_____ the acceptance and support.

_____ or, _____

YOUR THERAPIST

Take some time to think about what has been special to you about your therapist.

What I will miss most about _____ **is**

◆

"Don's wry humor always disarms me. Once when I was carrying on and predicting the worst for my son, he suggested that I put him on a preventative dose of Thorazine to fend off what was clearly an impending psychosis. That snapped me back to reality faster than any reassurance would have. I loved the glint in his eye when he said that. No one else has been able to make me laugh when I'm so full of anxiety."

"All of the good things that happened in therapy don't count for anything now because I am so mad at Dr. M. I hate him for moving and leaving me behind. He says that I'll remember the rest later, but I'm not so sure."

"Even when Dr. H challenged me and confronted my stuff, I always knew he liked and respected me. He'd hang in there with me. Who will do that for me once therapy is over?"

"I will miss Emily's nurturing qualities. I never want to forget how it felt when she gave me a hug. I felt so safe and protected."

◆

YOUR FORMER SELF

Change can involve a sense of loss as we give up old ways of coping, feeling, thinking, and behaving. Even though the new ways may be more positive and life enhancing, we may feel sad (see page 126, "Obstacles to Change"). Do you feel that you have lost an important part of you as a result of therapy?

When I think about how I used to be, I miss

◆

"There was something beautiful about the naive, trusting way that I approached life. Sure, I got stepped on, but I had a kind of innocence that is gone."

"It's hard to explain, but having decided to live and to give up the option of suicide is a loss to me. It was like a friend that could always be there as a last resort."

◆

YOUR UNREALISTIC EXPECTATIONS

As you have thought about your gains, you may have been struck also by what you have not accomplished. Ending therapy brings us face to face with our limitations. We may have wanted to be liked by everyone, free of tumultuous feelings, unseemly behavior, or difficult daily problems. Therapy just cannot make us the ideal people we may have secretly hoped to become. Ending therapy challenges us to accept our imperfections and like who we are.

I have given up my expectation that

◆

"My mother will never love me the way that I want her to and no amount of work in therapy will change that reality."

"When I began therapy, I was sure that ultimately it would help me be a serene person, calm with my husband and kids, wise beyond my years. I think I am smarter now in a certain way, but serene? No way, there are no flies on me. I'm more outspoken and passionate than I was before. Goodbye to that serene image. It's just not who I am."

◆

Anticipate Future Hard Times

Everything cannot be tied up neatly. You can be sure that life will present you with the unexpected. Yet you may be able to foresee some issues that may be hard for you to deal with after therapy.

An old problem may recur or an event may stir up some difficulty. You may be graduating from college, having your youngest leave the nest or dealing with the death of a parent in the foreseeable future. You may worry that a particular emotional issue may recur. Imagine your future vulnerable moments and explore them in therapy now to prepare for them.

What may be hard for me in the future is

What I can do to help myself through

I might return to therapy if

◆

"My therapist and I figured out that because I survived the terrorism in my country and left everyone I love behind to suffer, I feel guilty and depressed whenever something good happens to me. I will be getting my Ph.D. after I leave therapy and want to catch myself before I drift into another depression."

"I've worked as much as I can on the problem I have with men. I can't wait around in therapy until I meet someone. If I have trouble once I get into a serious relationship, I'll just come back."

◆

Set Goals

With your therapist's help, consider your goals for the future:

1. _____
2. _____
3. _____
4. _____

I can reach my goals by

◆ Task 4 ◆
Say Goodbye

Finally, after all is said and done, the time has come for you to say goodbye. Before you see your therapist for the ending session, let yourself fantasize about how you would like your last meeting to be and describe it in the space below.

Imagine what you would like to happen in this session. Picture what you would like from your therapist, from your fellow group members or partner in couple therapy. Describe what you would like to do or say.

Now the time has come actually to say goodbye. You may find that your last session is less eventful or more moving than you expected. Complete the sentences below to describe what actually happened.

In my last session I

In my last session my group or partner

In my last session my therapist

What I will always want to remember about my last session is

How I feel about having left therapy

◆

"Everyone in group recalled a piece of work that I had done and told me what they would miss about me. Then we had champagne."

"Our last session was melancholy. There were some silences. After talking about my hopes and sadness about leaving, we shook hands warmly."

"I gave my therapist a new plant for her office and told her how grateful I was for all her care and attention."

◆

·12·
After Therapy

TASKS

1. Be Your Own Therapist
2. Explore Other Routes to Emotional Well-Being
3. Continue Using This Book

What can you do to continue building on the gains you made during therapy? The learning and growing that begin in therapy constitute a lifelong process. Successful therapy provides us with the knowledge and tools to deal in new and better ways with life's challenges. We can continue to employ what we have learned long after we have said goodbye to our therapists. We can also develop new resources to help us resolve problems creatively and promote our well-being. This chapter offers guidance to make the most of your life after therapy.

◆ Task 1 ◆
Be Your Own Therapist

As you contend with life on your own, you'll find many opportunities to apply the lessons you learned in therapy. It is your job now to provide for yourself what therapy once provided for you. And you may find—perhaps unexpectedly—that you are good at it.

The following statements represent aspects of what your therapist might do for you. Check those that describe how you are doing at being your own therapist, and write a sentence or two if you wish at the end of each statement.

_____ I make time to think about myself.

_____ I take my thoughts and feelings seriously.

_____ I can comfort myself.

_____ I avoid making harsh judgments about myself and others.

_____ I try to understand other people's point of view.

_____ I am pursuing my goals.

_____ I make an effort to see the part I play in any problems that I have.

_____ When a problem occurs, I manage it.

_____ I work at understanding what I think or feel.

_____ I am optimistic about solving future problems.

_____ or, _____

As we take stock of ourselves after therapy, we may be doing just fine; we handle our affairs, manage good and bad days, and deal with life's ups and downs. The experience of therapy has helped equip us to deal with whatever comes our way.

Even the most successful therapy cannot change hard realities; we all experience some rough times in our lives. You may have trouble coping with an old psychological issue you hoped had been resolved in therapy. Perhaps an unexpected challenge or difficulty has emerged, and you are unsure how to make things better. Your experience in therapy can provide a model for how you can help yourself now.

Have a Therapy Session with Yourself

If you get stuck, take some time and engage in a therapy session with yourself. Use this special time to think about how your therapist might have helped. Give yourself what your therapist would have offered you during a session. Recapturing your therapist's actual approach can help you understand and handle what's troubling you now.

During your session with yourself, put the tools for success in therapy into action (see page 137). Be curious about your problem, carefully observe yourself and the issue that concerns you, empathize with yourself and anyone else involved, and use good communication when the problem concerns another person. Think about the questions your therapist might ask you, and imagine the comments he or she might make.

If you have a problem right now, use the space below or your journal to write an imaginary dialogue between you and your former therapist. Describe the problem that bothers you, respond with your therapist's questions and your answers, and continue the imaginary dialogue in your journal until you reach some understanding or a possible solution.

How I might describe the problem to my therapist

How my therapist might respond

◆

"Whenever I'm stuck and can't resolve a messy situation, I go through the same process that I did in therapy. I tell myself that I have a good reason for staying stuck; I just don't know what it is yet. Then I begin writing down anything I can think of that would be a reason not to change, no matter how silly it seems."

"We made a plan in couples' therapy that if we start to get into a heated argument, we will take time out and write to each other in a special notebook. This plan has worked pretty well. We each get a chance to express ourselves, and I know that when I read what my husband has to say, I can attend to his ideas without being distracted by the anger on his face or in his voice. This technique we learned in therapy has kept us communicating through some hard times."

◆

If an issue, crisis, or problem comes up that is too difficult to handle on your own, you may want to touch base with therapy. Unlike the first time around, now you have a good idea of what therapy is like. In order to obtain some extra help, you may decide to consult with your former therapist or to contact a new one.

If you think returning to therapy means that therapy has failed and fear that your former therapist will be disappointed in you, you may hesitate. Keep in mind that many therapists enjoy keeping in touch with their clients, and all realize that hard times may bring a client back for a visit. A visit or two with your former therapist may help you sort through these issues. If you are considering seeing someone new, turn to page 59 for more information.

◆

"Two years after my analysis ended, I had an intense and prolonged anxiety attack in anticipation of the removal of a benign mole from my face. It took my analyst one interpretation in one session, and I was myself again."

"My sudden fear of AIDS is totally irrational, and getting information about it has not helped. Even though there's no way I've been exposed, I think about it all the time. I'm going back to therapy to find out what my anxiety is all about."

"In my three years of therapy, I was able to calm my fears about commitment and get married. During my wife's pregnancy, two years after therapy ended, I started to become very anxious and had recurrent nightmares about a newcomer in town who's trying to kill me. I returned to therapy to work on what it means to me to be a father—an issue that never came up before."

◆ Task 2 ◆
Explore Other Routes to
Emotional Well-Being

Good psychotherapy is an exciting, life-enhancing experience. It increases your creativity and your sense of what is possible. There are many ways to maintain the benefits of therapy and cope with new problems. You can find existing opportunities for exploration, self-expression, problem solving, and growth similar to those that therapy provided or you can create such situations yourself. Consider these other routes to emotional well-being.

◆ *Talk to someone you trust.* Some people are natural, intuitive helpers. Talk things over with a wise friend, a relative, or a spiritual adviser who can offer you a good ear and some gentle advice. You can also put together a support group of people in circumstances similar to your own. Simply sharing a difficulty with others may help.

You may want to schedule a regular time to talk with a special friend, your partner, or a support group. Set apart the meeting times as you would your therapy time.

◆ *Make changes in your life-style.* Time away from stressful activities or simply breaks from routine are refreshing and restore our depleted resources.

We can make an important contribution to our well-being by eating and sleeping well and exercising. If your body is tired, starving, or jolted with overdoses of sugar, caffeine, or tobacco, eventually you will feel bad. Exercise works in a number of ways. It provides a sense of accomplishment while calming and relaxing us. You look and feel better if you exercise.

◆ *Create meaningful opportunities.* Below is a list of activities that can provide some of what you used to have in therapy.

◆ *Take special care of yourself on a regular basis.* Be generous with yourself and make time for activities that are nurturing and gratifying. Treat yourself to something special from time to time.

◆ *Learn your family history.* Talk to relatives and reconstruct your family history. Notice repetitions of themes from generation to generation. Make a genogram (diagram of your family history), and write down your findings for the next generation.

◆ *Keep a dream log.* Regularly record your dreams to help you understand your inner life more deeply. Think about them in the way you learned in your therapy.

If this is a new area for you, consider keeping the dream log in the following way. Write your thoughts and feelings about the location and characters in each dream, and see whether they remind you of yourself, anyone in your adult life, or someone from your childhood. Try to locate and understand any themes in your dreams.

Or make a list of the animate and inanimate objects in your dream. With the understanding that each element in your dream is your creation and represents some part of yourself, choose any object and describe who you are and the function you serve. For example, you might choose to write a monologue from the point of view of a dog that appears in a dream. You would say: "I am the dog in _____'s dream. I am playful and long for attention. I am always looking for someone to care for me." To learn more about dreams, see "Resources," page 250.

• *Develop and pursue new interests.*   Participate in athletics, or take a course in something you have always wanted to learn. You might find meditation, movement, or dance therapy rewarding and helpful in reducing stress.

• *Volunteer.*   On a regular basis, give something of yourself to an organization or cause that is meaningful to you.

• *Join a self-help group.*   Self-help groups provide therapeutic experiences for people with similar problems and often have good records of success. Group members focus on a particular theme or problem, share experiences, and offer one another support. There is a self-help or support group for nearly every kind of issue; check "Resources," page 238, for some examples. Local Y's and church groups offer workshops on various subjects and may also house self-help groups.

• *Get special training, counseling, or planning assistance.*   A number of programs offer training or counseling in such areas as managing stress (relaxation training, yoga, hypnosis), becoming more assertive, financial management, selecting a career, or making the most of retirement.

• *Keep a journal.*   Throughout this book you have been encouraged to record your thoughts and feelings. Continuing the journal is a particularly good way to keep building on the gains that you have made in therapy. A journal provides a private and safe way to express and explore your thoughts and feelings. Writing down experiences, dreams, and fantasies promotes understanding and provides an opportunity to plan, keep track of your progress, and gain perspective.

◆ *Read books and articles.*   Many popular self-help books are written by thoughtful experts who share their insights and experience. Reading can provide new ideas, inspiration, and reassuring information.

An annotated bibliography of helpful books on a variety of topics can be found in the Resources section of this book.

◆ Task 3 ◆
Continue Using This Book

Although this book is not a replacement for therapy, it is here as a resource for you for as long as you need it. Rereading of relevant pages can act as a refresher course, reminding you of what you once knew.

Refer to the text for specific help, or use your handwritten responses to remember what it was like when you were in therapy. Pay special attention to those tasks that were particularly helpful the first time around. Here are some ideas of how you can continue using this book:

• *For help in understanding or managing a current problem.* Remember to use the Tools for Success: Curiosity, Powers of Observation, Empathy, Receptivity, and Clear Communication —pages 137–148.
• *If you cannot figure out what is bothering you.*   Take stock, Chapter 1 to pinpoint what may be troubling you. Reread Task 2 in Chapter 7 on overcoming obstacles to change. Note if you are restricting yourself with self-defeating beliefs. Reading page 126 will help you set priorities to reduce your distress.
• *If you are having a hard time in a relationship.*   Check the sections on building a relationship with your therapist, pages 79 and 116. See what lessons you can apply to your current relationship.
• *To facilitate decision making if your problems are getting too much for you to handle on your own.*   Read Chapter 2 to help you decide whether to return to therapy.
• *If you are getting ready to make a leap forward.*   Reread the quotes throughout the book. Someone may have said something that strikes a chord.

By giving yourself the kind of care and attention that your therapist accorded you and by using the tools and strategies you learned in therapy, you can handle your daily life well, continue to overcome any problems that emerge, and build on the gains that you made.

This book has helped you to become an active, aware participant in the therapy process. By helping you master a series of tasks and by teaching you to be aware of what works for you and what does not, it enabled you to learn and grow.

You have seen that by breaking down a large task into small steps, you can accomplish a lot. You could walk across the entire country by taking one step at a time. Don't stop now. Continue your journey of self-exploration and growth throughout your life.

•Appendix•
When Someone You Care About Needs Help

How to Tell Someone That You Think
   He or She Needs Help
Does Your Child Need Therapy?
Does Your Aging Parent Need Therapy?
When Someone You Care About Needs a Consultation

◆ How to Tell Someone That You Think He or She Needs Help ◆

It is hard to see someone we care about in distress. We want to help, but often we don't know what to do or are afraid that we might make things worse. This chapter focuses on how to decide if someone has a problem best addressed by therapy, and how you can be effective in seeing that he or she gets help.

The next exercises help you put your finger on what is troubling you about the person.

I think _____ may need therapy because he or she

_____ is doing badly at work or school.
_____ is talking about suicide.

_____ is a danger to others.

_____ is coping poorly with a difficult life circumstance.

_____ is having trouble thinking clearly.

_____ is self-defeating.

_____ is threatening others with harm.

_____ lacks self-confidence.

_____ is violent.

_____ has troublesome relationship(s).

_____ is pessimistic or unrealistic about his or her ability to cope.

_____ is abusing drugs, alcohol, or food.

_____ is (sad) (angry) (anxious) (distressed) (agitated) (out of control) (panicked) (dissatisfied).

_____ complains about the same problems without doing anything about them.

_____ keeps getting into the same messy situations, without any idea of how to avoid or resolve them.

_____ feels awful about him / herself.

_____ has sudden mood swings.

_____ wants to change.

_____ has sleep difficulties.

_____ can't get along with friends.

_____ keeps getting into trouble with authorities.

_____ wants help.

_____ or, _____

Since none of us is perfect, it can be very uncomfortable to tell someone that you think he or she needs help. You may worry that your friend or family member will be embarrassed or angry or will blame you as the bearer of unwelcome news. Nevertheless, taking a chance and expressing your concern may be a turning point, providing the push the person needs to get help. Here are some guidelines to help you think about what to say and how to say it.

Guidelines for a Caring Confrontation

• **Be direct.** Even if your loved one reacts defensively at first, talk directly about the problem you see. Direct communication invites serious consideration; indirect approaches can confuse, frighten, and isolate your loved one.

When a Foreigner

When a foreigner who is not of thy people Israel

shall come from a far country for thy name's sake

—for they shall hear of thy great name, and of thy mighty hand,

    and of thine outstretched arm—

when he shall come and pray toward this house;

hear thou in heaven, thy dwelling place,

and do according to all for which the foreigner calleth to thee;

that all the peoples of the earth may know thy name and fear

    thee, as doth thy people Israel,

and that they may know that this house which I have built

is called by thy name.

ZION

וגם אל הנכרי

וְגַם אֶל־הַנָּכְרִי אֲשֶׁר לֹא־מֵעַמְּךָ יִשְׂרָאֵל הוּא

וּבָא מֵאֶרֶץ רְחוֹקָה לְמַעַן שְׁמֶךָ.

כִּי יִשְׁמְעוּן אֶת־שִׁמְךָ הַגָּדוֹל וְאֶת־יָדְךָ הַחֲזָקָה וּזְרֹעֲךָ הַנְּטוּיָה

וּבָא וְהִתְפַּלֵּל אֶל־הַבַּיִת הַזֶּה.

אַתָּה תִּשְׁמַע הַשָּׁמַיִם מְכוֹן שִׁבְתֶּךָ

וְעָשִׂיתָ כְּכֹל אֲשֶׁר־יִקְרָא אֵלֶיךָ הַנָּכְרִי

לְמַעַן יֵדְעוּן כָּל־עַמֵּי הָאָרֶץ אֶת־שְׁמֶךָ לְיִרְאָה אֹתְךָ כְּעַמְּךָ יִשְׂרָאֵל

וְלָדַעַת כִּי־שִׁמְךָ נִקְרָא

עַל־הַבַּיִת הַזֶּה אֲשֶׁר בָּנִיתִי.

Leave Us Not

Though our iniquities testify against us,

act, O Lord, for thy name's sake;

for our backslidings are many,

we have sinned against thee.

O thou hope of Israel,

its savior in time of trouble,

why shouldst thou be like a stranger in the land,

like a wayfarer who turns aside to tarry for a night?

Why shouldst thou be like a man confused,

like a mighty man who cannot save?

Yet thou, O Lord, art in the midst of us,

and we are called by thy name;

leave us not.

אל תניחנו

אִם־עֲוֹנֵינוּ עָנוּ בָנוּ
יְהוָה עֲשֵׂה לְמַעַן שְׁמֶךָ
כִּי־רַבּוּ מְשׁוּבֹתֵינוּ
לְךָ חָטָאנוּ.
מִקְוֵה יִשְׂרָאֵל
מוֹשִׁיעוֹ בְּעֵת צָרָה
לָמָּה תִהְיֶה כְּגֵר בָּאָרֶץ
וּכְאֹרֵחַ נָטָה לָלוּן.
לָמָּה תִהְיֶה כְּאִישׁ נִדְהָם
כְּגִבּוֹר לֹא־יוּכַל לְהוֹשִׁיעַ
וְאַתָּה בְקִרְבֵּנוּ יְהוָה
וְשִׁמְךָ עָלֵינוּ נִקְרָא
אַל־תַּנִּחֵנוּ.

Thy City and Thy People

O my God, incline thy ear and hear,

open thy eyes and behold our desolation,

and the city which is called by thy name;

for we do not present our supplications before thee on the
    ground of our righteousness,

but on the ground of thy great mercy.

O Lord, hear;

O Lord, forgive;

O Lord, give heed and act, delay not;

for thy own sake, O my God,

because thy city and thy people are called by thy name.

על עירך ועל עמך

הַטֵּה אֱלֹהַי אָזְנְךָ וּשְׁמָע
פְּקַח עֵינֶיךָ וּרְאֵה שֹׁמְמֹתֵינוּ
וְהָעִיר אֲשֶׁר־נִקְרָא שִׁמְךָ עָלֶיהָ
כִּי לֹא עַל־צִדְקֹתֵינוּ אֲנַחְנוּ מַפִּילִים תַּחֲנוּנֵינוּ לְפָנֶיךָ
כִּי עַל־רַחֲמֶיךָ הָרַבִּים.
אֲדֹנָי שְׁמָעָה
אֲדֹנָי סְלָחָה
אֲדֹנָי הַקְשִׁיבָה וַעֲשֵׂה אַל־תְּאַחַר
לְמַעַנְךָ אֱלֹהַי
כִּי־שִׁמְךָ נִקְרָא עַל־עִירְךָ וְעַל־עַמֶּךָ.

Jerusalem, Thou Holy City

Blessed be God that liveth forever,

and blessed be His kingdom,

for He chastiseth, and hath mercy.

He leadeth down to Sheol and He bringeth up again;

neither is there any that can escape His hand.

Give thanks unto Him before the nations, ye children of Israel,

for He hath scattered you among them.

There proclaim ye His greatness,

extol Him before all the living:

for He is our Lord and God,

He is our Father forever.

I will extol my God,

and my soul shall praise the King of heaven.

O Jerusalem, thou holy city! He will chastise thee for the works

    of thy children,

and will have mercy again on the sons of the righteous.

Blessed are they that love thee,

for they shall rejoice in thy peace.

Blessed are they that have been sorrowful for all thy chastise-

    ments,

for they shall rejoice in thee,

and see all thy glory and be glad forever.

Let my soul bless God the great King.

ירושלים קריה קדושה

בָּרוּךְ אֱלֹהִים חַי־עוֹלָמִים
וּבְרוּכָה מַלְכוּתוֹ
כִּי הוּא מְיַסֵּר וּמְרַחֵם
מוֹרִיד שְׁאוֹל וַיָּעַל
וְאֵין נִמְלָט מִיָּדוֹ.
הוֹדוּ לוֹ בְּנֵי יִשְׂרָאֵל לְעֵינֵי הַגּוֹיִם
כִּי־הוּא הֵפִיץ אוֹתָנוּ בְתוֹכָם.
שָׁם תַּגִּידוּ גְדֻלָּתוֹ
רוֹמְמוּ אוֹתוֹ לְעֵינֵי כָל־חָי
כִּי־הוּא אֲדוֹנֵינוּ וֵאלֹהֵינוּ
הוּא אָבִינוּ לְעוֹלָם וָעֶד.

אֲרוֹמֵם אֶת־אֱלֹהַי
וְנַפְשִׁי לְמֶלֶךְ הַשָּׁמַיִם תָּרָנֵּן גְּדֻלָּתוֹ.
יְרוּשָׁלַיִם קִרְיָה קְדוֹשָׁה הוּא יְיַסְּרֵךְ עַל מַעֲשֵׂי בָנַיִךְ
וְיָשׁוּב וִירַחֵם עַל־בְּנֵי הַצַּדִּיקִים.

אַשְׁרֵי אוֹהֲבַיִךְ
עוֹד יִשְׂמְחוּ בִשְׁלוֹמֵךְ.
אַשְׁרֵי הַנֶּעֱצָבִים עַל־כָּל־מַכּוֹתַיִךְ
כִּי יִשְׂמְחוּ עָלַיִךְ
בִּרְאוֹתָם אֶת־כָּל־כְּבוֹדֵךְ וְיָגִילוּ לְעוֹלָם
בָּרְכִי נַפְשִׁי אֶת־הָאֱלֹהִים אֶת־הַמֶּלֶךְ הַגָּדוֹל.

Take Pity, O Lord

Take pity, O Lord our God, on us
and on Israel, thy folk,
and on Jerusalem, thy city,
and on Mount Zion, thy glory's habitation,
and on the great and holy house,
over which thy name is called.

Our Father, shepherd us,
feed us, maintain us,
sustain us, ease us,
pray ease us speedily from all our troubles.

Nor let us be needing, O Lord our God,
gifts at the hands of flesh-and-blood,
nor loans at the hands of those
whose gift is petty, humiliation much;

but at thy hand
that is full and broad,
and rich and open;
that we be not shamed in this world
nor disgraced in the other.

And the kingship of the house of David, thine anointed,
return to its place,
speedily in our days.

רחם

רַחֵם יְיָ אֱלֹהֵינוּ עָלֵינוּ

וְעַל יִשְׂרָאֵל עַמֶּךָ

וְעַל יְרוּשָׁלַיִם עִירָךְ

וְעַל הַר צִיּוֹן מִשְׁכַּן כְּבוֹדָךְ

וְעַל הַבַּיִת הַגָּדוֹל וְהַקָּדוֹשׁ

שֶׁנִּקְרָא שִׁמְךָ עָלָיו.

אָבִינוּ רְעֵנוּ

זוּנֵנוּ פַּרְנְסֵנוּ

כַּלְכְּלֵנוּ הַרְוִיחֵנוּ

הַרְוַח לָנוּ מְהֵרָה מִכָּל צָרוֹתֵינוּ.

וְאַל תַּצְרִיכֵנוּ יְיָ אֱלֹהֵינוּ

לֹא לִידֵי מַתְּנוֹת בָּשָׂר וָדָם

וְלֹא לִידֵי הַלְוָאָתָם

שֶׁמַּתְּנָתָם מְעוּטָה וְחֶרְפָּתָם מְרֻבָּה

אֶלָּא לְיָדְךָ

הַמְּלֵאָה וְהָרְחָבָה

הָעֲשִׁירָה וְהַפְּתוּחָה

שֶׁלֹּא נֵבוֹשׁ בָּעוֹלָם הַזֶּה

וְלֹא נִכָּלֵם לְעוֹלָם הַבָּא.

וּמַלְכוּת בֵּית דָּוִד מְשִׁיחָךְ

תַּחֲזִירֶנָּה לִמְקוֹמָהּ

בִּמְהֵרָה בְיָמֵינוּ.

Comfort, O Lord

Comfort, O Lord our God,

the mourners of Zion,

and the mourners of Jerusalem,

and the city desolate in her mourning:

For the exile of her sons,

the ruin of her home,

the passing of her glory,

the loss of her people.

She sitteth with her head covered

like a barren woman who hath not borne.

Legions overran her,

aliens possessed her:

They have put thy people Israel to the sword,

and in wilfulness have slain God's faithful.

Therefore let Zion weep bitterly,

and Jerusalem give forth her voice.

My heart, my heart goes out for the slain!

My very inwards churn for the slain!

Thou, O Lord, didst consume her with fire;

and with fire thou wilt in future rebuild her.

As it is said,

נַחֵם יְיָ אֱלֹהֵינוּ

אֶת־אֲבֵלֵי צִיּוֹן

וְאֶת־אֲבֵלֵי יְרוּשָׁלַיִם

וְאֶת־הָעִיר הָאֲבֵלָה וְהֶחָרֵבָה

וְהַבְּזוּיָה וְהַשּׁוֹמֵמָה.

הָאֲבֵלָה מִבְּלִי בָנֶיהָ

וְהֶחָרֵבָה מִמְּעוֹנוֹתֶיהָ

וְהַבְּזוּיָה מִכְּבוֹדָהּ

וְהַשּׁוֹמֵמָה מֵאֵין יוֹשֵׁב.

וְהִיא יוֹשֶׁבֶת וְרֹאשָׁהּ חָפוּי

כְּאִשָּׁה עֲקָרָה שֶׁלֹּא יָלָדָה.

וַיְבַלְּעוּהָ לְגִיוֹנוֹת

וַיִּירָשׁוּהָ עוֹבְדֵי זָרִים

וַיַּטִּילוּ אֶת־עַמְּךָ יִשְׂרָאֵל לֶחָרֶב

וַיַּהַרְגוּ בְזָדוֹן חֲסִידֵי עֶלְיוֹן.

עַל־כֵּן צִיּוֹן בְּמַר תִּבְכֶּה

וִירוּשָׁלַיִם תִּתֵּן קוֹלָהּ.

לִבִּי לִבִּי עַל חַלְלֵיהֶם

מֵעַי מֵעַי עַל חַלְלֵיהֶם.

כִּי אַתָּה יְיָ בָּאֵשׁ הִצַּתָּהּ

וּבָאֵשׁ אַתָּה עָתִיד לִבְנוֹתָהּ.

כָּאָמוּר

237

"As for me, I will be unto her, saith the Lord, a wall of fire
    round about,
and I will be a glory in the midst of her."
Blessed art thou, O Lord,
who comfortest Zion
and rebuildest Jerusalem.

וַאֲנִי אֶהְיֶה־לָּה נְאֻם־יְיָ חוֹמַת אֵשׁ סָבִיב

וּלְכָבוֹד אֶהְיֶה בְתוֹכָהּ.

בָּרוּךְ אַתָּה יְיָ

מְנַחֵם צִיּוֹן

וּבוֹנֵה יְרוּשָׁלָיִם.

From a Judaeo-Greek Lament

O my God who art on high

in the heavens above,

look thou upon Israel,

which is in exile.

Look and be kindly disposed to us,

and console us.

Let not our eyes look

longer upon exile.

I beg thee, my Lord,

a thousand times I kneel before thee.

Conduct us to our Messiah

in holy Jerusalem.

אוכו   אותמו פו אישי שטאפשׁילַה / שׁטוש אורַנוש אַפַנו   אא

אוכו   יַאידַשׁטו ישׂרַאֵל / פוני שׁטין אֶקסוריַא   אא

אוכו   יַאידשׁ קֵי קַלימוניסומַשׁ / קֵי פַריגוריסמַס   אא

אוכו   נַמין אידון פְליו טַמַטיַימַס / פִּיליו טין אֶקסוריַיה   אא

אוכו   פַרַקַלושֵׁי קירַימו / קיליַיה פְרוסקינוסֵׁי   אא

אוכו   פְרובודישֵׁמַשׁ טו מַשׁיח מַס / אישׁטין אַיַיה ירושַלַים   אא

ΏΧΟΥ   ῏Ω ΘΈ ΜΟΥ ΠΟῪ ΕΪΣΑΙ ΣΤᾺ ΨΗΛΆ

Ὢχου	῏Ω θέ μου ποῦ εἶσαι στὰ ψηλά στοὺς ὀρανοὺς ἀπάνου	αα
Ὢχου	Γιὰ ἰδὲς τὸ Ἰσραελ ποῦ ʾναι στὴν ἐξουρία	αα
Ὢχου	Γιὰ ἰδὲς καὶ καλλιμονησοῦ μᾶς καὶ παρηγόρισε μᾶς	αα
Ὢχου	Νὰ μὴν ἰδοῦν πλιὸ τὰ μάτιά μας πλιὸ τὴν ἐξουρία	αα
Ὢχου	Παρακαλῶ σὲ κύριέ μου κίλια προσκυνῶ σέ	αα
Ὢχου	Προβόδισε μᾶς τὸ Μασιαχ μας εἰς τὴν ἄγια Ἰερουσαλημ	αα

The Sanctity of Zion

Master of the universe, make it your care that our heart, our thought, be knotted and bound to your sacredness.

Let us be worthy and our mind enlightened, that we may understand your sanctity; sweet to us may the sanctity be of the holy land where from eternity you have made your sanctity rest, over against a Land of Israel that lies in heaven.

You have chosen that land from all the world, that your presence may rest therein; and the prayers from abroad journey by way of the Land of Israel and by way of Jerusalem and by way of the Holy of Holies—that is the journey all prayers make to you.

די קדושה פון דעם הייליגין לאנד

רבונו של עולם, גיב אונזר הארץ, אונזר מחשבה, זאל אן
גיקניפט און באהעפפט ווערין אן דיין הייליגקייט,

מיר זאלין זוכה זיין דער לייכטין אונזר שכל, מיר זאלין פר
שטיין דיא קדושה, און עס זאל אונז זיין זיס דיא קדושה פון דעם
הייליגין לאנד וואס דוא האשט פון אייביג אהן דיין קדושה
גימאכט רוען דערינן, און אנקעגין ארץ ישראל וואס עס שטייט
אין הימל.

דוא האשט אויש דער ווילט דאס לאנד פון גאר דער וועלט צו
רוען דיין שכינה דערינן, און דיא תפילות פון חוץ לארץ גייהין
דרך ארץ ישראל און דרך ירושלים, און דרך דעם קדשי
הקדשים גיין אלע תפילות צו דיר.

O God, Save Masada

Steady, O God, the footsteps of those who have slipped off the
gallows
In strange lands, and have risen upon the walls of the fortress;
Steady them that they may not stumble and fall, for weary they
are, and still stagger.

Soften the hard rocks of Masada under their heads when they
do fatigue:
Do not let the cold hail of despair blast that which they have
sown here, the seed of souls and of dreams.
Bid, O God, many rains of solace to fall upon it, and may the
dew fructify it at night,
Till it be rewarded with the promise of harvest.

For if this time again you will not be merciful, O God,
Nor accept our dream, nor heed the offerings of those who strive
to make the dream come true—
O God, save Masada.

אלהים נצור מסדה

לַאֲשֶׁר נִשְׁמְטוּ מִתְּלִיּוֹת־נֶכֶר וַיַּעֲלוּ אֶל הַחוֹמָה –
הָכֵן צַעֲדָם, אֱלֹהִים, לְבַל יִמְעֲדוּ, לִבְלִי יִפֹּלוּ
כִּי עוֹד כּוֹשְׁלִים הֵם וַעֲיֵפִים.

רַכֵּךְ סַלְעֵי מַסָּדָה קָשִׁים לְמַרְאֲשׁוֹתֵיהֶם כִּי יִיעָפוּ!
לַאֲשֶׁר בְּדִמְעָה זָרְעוּ פֹּה זֶרַע נֶפֶשׁ וַחֲלוֹמוֹת –
אַל יַכֵּהוּ בְרַד הַיָּגוֹן, אַל יְיַבְּשׁוּהוּ חַמְסִינֵי־פִּתְאֹם,
צַוֵּה אֶל גִּשְׁמֵי־נֹחַם רַבִּים וְיַפְרֵהוּ טַל בַּלֵּילוֹת
עֲדֵי יָנוּב לִקְצִיר שְׁלוּמִים!

אִם גַּם הַפַּעַם, אֱלֹהִים, לֹא תָחֹן וְאֶת הַחֲלוֹם לֹא תְרַצֶּה
וְלִקְרְבָּנוֹת פּוֹתְרָיו לֹא תִשְׁעֶה גַּם עַתָּה –
אֱלֹהִים, נְצוֹר מַסָּדָה.

245

Before the Battle

Grant a blessing for our boys—for the time has come.
See them silent and ready—and their eyes glow.
See, evening falls, wind in the tree-tops. The pine quivers.
There'll be battle tonight. And they are very few.

Bless them, my Lord. For the time has come.
Stars are lit and many camps gather yonder.

For who shall see daylight? And who shall fall and die?
Shall victory be gained or defeat and the grave?

Bless them, my Lord, bless the fighting-men.
Bless their weapons lest they miss... bless their homes.
Bless this people, its youths and fighters,
Until the battle be done.

They have just left silently and their footsteps fade,
Heavy murk and night in the mountains,
Bless them—for the time has come.
Grant a blessing for our boys.

קְרָב יְהִי הַלֵּיל

הָבֵא בְּרָכָה לַנְּעָרִים – כִּי בָּאָה עֵת.
רְאֵה אוֹתָם שׁוֹתְקִים וּנְכוֹנִים – וְעֵינֵיהֶם דּוֹלְקוֹת.
רְאֵה יוֹרֵד הָעֶרֶב, רוּחַ בַּצַּמָּרוֹת, הָאָרֶץ מְרַטֵּט.
קְרָב יְהִי הַלֵּיל. וְהֵמָּה מְעַטִּים מְאֹד.

בָּרְכֵם, אֵלִי, כִּי בָּאָה עֵת.
כּוֹכָבִים הֵצִיתוּ וּמַחֲנוֹת רַבִּים נֶאֱסָפִים מֵעֵבֶר.

כִּי מִי יִרְאֶה אוֹר-יוֹם? וּמִי נָפַל וָמֵת?
הַנִּצָּחוֹן יֻשַּׂג אוֹ אִם תְּבוּסָה וָקֶבֶר?

בָּרְכֵם, אֵלִי, בָּרֵךְ יוֹצְאֵי לַמִּלְחָמָה.
בָּרֵךְ נִשְׁקָם לְבַל יַחֲטִיא... בָּרֵךְ בֵּיתָם.
בָּרֵךְ אֶת זֶה הָעָם, אֶת נְעָרָיו וְלוֹחֲמָיו,
עַד קְרָב יִתַּם.

הִנֵּה יָצְאוּ שְׁקֵטִים וְצַעֲדָם אוֹבֵד,
וַעֲלָטָה כְּבֵדָה וְלֵיל בֶּהָרִים,
בָּרְכֵם – כִּי בָּאָה עֵת.
הָבֵא בְּרָכָה לַנְּעָרִים.

The Return

Let our eyes behold
thy return in mercy
to Zion.
Blessed art thou, O Lord,
who restorest thy presence
to Zion.

ותחזינה עינינו

וְתֶחֱזֶינָה עֵינֵינוּ
בְּשׁוּבְךָ לְצִיּוֹן
בְּרַחֲמִים.
בָּרוּךְ אַתָּה יְיָ
הַמַּחֲזִיר שְׁכִינָתוֹ
לְצִיּוֹן.

SABBATH

Accept Our Rest

Our God and God of our fathers,

accept our rest.

Give us through thy commandments a sense of the holy

and let us share in the knowledge of thy Word.

Fill us with thy goodness,

make us joyful with thy help.

Cleanse our hearts to serve thee truly.

Through thy love and grace, O Lord our God,

may thy holy Sabbath become our own;

may Israel rest that day and hallow thy name.

רצה במנוחתנו

אֱלֹהֵינוּ וֵאלֹהֵי אֲבוֹתֵינוּ
רְצֵה בִמְנוּחָתֵנוּ.
קַדְּשֵׁנוּ בְּמִצְוֹתֶיךָ
וְתֵן חֶלְקֵנוּ בְּתוֹרָתֶךָ.
שַׂבְּעֵנוּ מִטּוּבֶךָ
וְשַׂמְּחֵנוּ בִּישׁוּעָתֶךָ
וְטַהֵר לִבֵּנוּ לְעָבְדְּךָ בֶּאֱמֶת.
וְהַנְחִילֵנוּ יְיָ אֱלֹהֵינוּ
בְּאַהֲבָה וּבְרָצוֹן שַׁבַּת קָדְשֶׁךָ.
וְיָנוּחוּ בָהּ יִשְׂרָאֵל מְקַדְּשֵׁי שְׁמֶךָ.

Blessed Be the Name

Blessed be the name of the Lord of the universe.

Blessed be thy crown and thy abiding-place.

May thy favor ever be with the people of Israel.

Reveal to thy people in thy sanctuary the redeeming power of
    thy right hand.

Give unto us the good gift of thy light,

and in mercy accept our prayers.

Thou feedest and sustainest us;

thou rulest over all;

thou rulest over kings,

for the kingdom is thine.

Not in man do I put my trust,

nor upon any angel do I rely,

but only upon the God of heaven,

who is the God of truth,

and whose Torah is truth,

and whose prophets are prophets of truth,

and who aboundeth in deeds of goodness and truth.

In Him do I trust,

and unto His holy and glorious name I utter praises.

May it be thy will

דְּתִפְתַּח לִבִּי בְּאוֹרַיְתָא
וְתַשְׁלִים מִשְׁאֲלִין דְּלִבָּאִי
וְלִבָּא דְכָל־עַמָּךְ יִשְׂרָאֵל
לְטַב וּלְחַיִּין וְלִשְׁלָם.

Lord of All Eons

Lord of all eons, of zone upon zone,
High above other thrones you have your throne!
Marvel of might, whom the mighty have shown
Awe turned to praises in word and in tone.

You who have planned and created each thing,
Beast of the field and the bird on the wing,
Earthlings and angels unearthly, I sing
Morning and evening to you, Lord alone.

Lord of the mighty! yoke of the proud!
Great are your deeds, O staff of the bowed.
One who would fathom you—were he allowed
Thousands of years, you could never be known!

God whom the glories of spheres overtide,
Succor your lamb from the lion, and guide
Out of their exile the faithful, the tried
People you chose from the world as your own.

Deign to return to your Temple again!
Spirit and heart will arise to your plane,
Dancers will move to a lilting refrain
In the town of Jerusalem, fairer is none!

יה רבון עלם

יָהּ רִבּוֹן עָלַם וְעָלְמַיָּא
אַנְתְּ הוּא מַלְכָּא מֶלֶךְ מַלְכַיָּא
עוֹבַד גְּבוּרְתֵּךְ וְתִמְהַיָּא
שַׁפִּיר קֳדָמָךְ לְהַחֲוָיָה.

שְׁבָחִין אֲסַדֵּר צַפְרָא וְרַמְשָׁא
לָךְ אֱלָהָא קַדִּישָׁא דִּי בְרָא כָל־נַפְשָׁא
עִירִין קַדִּישִׁין וּבְנֵי אֱנָשָׁא
חֵיוַת בָּרָא וְעוֹפֵי שְׁמַיָּא.

רַבְרְבִין עוֹבְדָיךְ וְתַקִּיפִין
מָכֵךְ רָמַיָּא זַקֵּף כְּפִיפִין
לוּ יְחֵא גְבַר שְׁנִין אַלְפִין
לָא יֵעַל גְּבוּרְתֵּךְ בְּחֻשְׁבְּנָא.

אֱלָהָא דִּי לֵהּ יְקַר וּרְבוּתָא
פְּרֹק יָת־עָנָךְ מִפֻּם אַרְיָוָתָא
וְאַפֵּק יָת־עַמָּךְ מִגּוֹא גָלוּתָא
עַמָּךְ דִּי בְחַרְתְּ מִכָּל־אֻמַּיָּא.

לְמִקְדָּשָׁךְ תּוּב וּלְקֹדֶשׁ קֻדְשִׁין
אֲתַר דִּי בֵהּ יֶחֱדוּן רוּחִין וְנַפְשִׁין
וִיזַמְּרוּן שִׁירִין וְרַחֲשִׁין
בִּירוּשְׁלֵם קַרְתָּא דִי־שֻׁפְרַיָּא.

A Meditation before the Conclusion of the Sabbath

Creator of the world,

in your great mercy you have given us the holy Sabbath as a
     precious gift;

we are unable to thank you enough for this great bounty.

It is hard to take leave of the holy day.

We pray, merciful Father,

that the holiness of the Sabbath lead us to sacred thoughts, to a
     saintly life, untainted by sin.

Through the observance of the Sabbath may we merit good
     health, honorable sustenance, and may our children bring
     us joy.

May we be able to receive the next Sabbath in holiness,

and in its time—the day of redemption that is wholly a Sabbath.

א תחינה פאר הבדלה

באשעפער פון דער וועלט
מיט דיין גרויסין חסד האסטו אונז גיגעבן דעם טייערין פרזיענט
דעם שבת קודש.
מיר זיינען ניט אימשטאנד דיר צו דאנקען דער פאר וויל דאס
איז זייער אגרויסע מתנה.
און דרום איז אונז שווער צו שיידען זיך מיט דעם הייליגען שבת.
בעטין מיר דיר ערבארמיגער פאטער
אז די קדושה פון שבת זאל משפיע זיין אויף אונז מחשבות
קדושות אז מיר זאלען זיך האלטען הייליג און ריין פון זינד.
און בזכות השבת זאלסטו אונז געבען גיזונד און פרנסה בכבוד
און נחת אויף אונזערע קינדר.
און מיר זאלען זוכה זיין אנצונעמעז מיט הייליגקייט דעם
קומנדיגען שבת
און נאכהער ליום שכולו שבת.

Who Sets Apart the Sacred and Profane

Who sets apart the sacred and profane,
May He have mercy on our sins, and deign
To multiply our seed and what we gain,
Like sand, like stars by night.

The palm spins out her shadow, day has waned,
I call to God who holds me in His hands,
The watchman said, the morning cometh and
The night—also the night!

I call upon you, God, to help me know
The path of life that you would have me go,
To raise me from my lowly state, to show
Your grace from dawn to night.

Oh, make me clean of my iniquity,
So none may ask, to vex and sadden me,
Where is this God who wrought you? Where is He
Whose word is song by night!

For in your hand we are no more than clay!
Forgive the grave transgression and the slight,
And tidings will speed forth from day to day,
Resound from night to night.

המבדיל

הַמַּבְדִּיל בֵּין קֹדֶשׁ לְחוֹל
חַטֹּאתֵינוּ יִמְחֹל
זַרְעֵנוּ וְכַסְפֵּנוּ יַרְבֶּה כַחוֹל
וְכַכּוֹכָבִים בַּלָּיְלָה.

יוֹם פָּנָה כְּצֵל תֹּמֶר
אֶקְרָא לָאֵל עָלַי גֹּמֵר
אָמַר שׁוֹמֵר אָתָא בֹקֶר
וְגַם־לָיְלָה.

קְרָאתִיךָ יָהּ הוֹשִׁיעֵנִי
אֹרַח חַיִּים תּוֹדִיעֵנִי
מִדַּלָּה תְבַצְּעֵנִי
מִיּוֹם עַד לָיְלָה.

טַהֵר טִנּוּף מַעֲשַׂי
פֶּן יֹאמְרוּ מַכְעִיסַי
אַיֵּה אֱלוֹהַּ עֹשָׂי
נֹתֵן זְמִירוֹת בַּלָּיְלָה.

נַחְנוּ בְיָדְךָ כַּחֹמֶר
סְלַח נָא עַל קַל וָחֹמֶר
יוֹם לְיוֹם יַבִּיעַ אֹמֶר
וְלַיְלָה לְלָיְלָה.

God of Abraham

God of Abraham, of Isaac, and of Jacob,
Protect your dear people of Israel with your love.

The good and holy Sabbath nears its end,
Now turn to us in tenderness, and send
A happy week, abrim
With life and health, with bread and savor.
Let us be pure and righteous, grant your favor,
Untarnished gains and greater strength of limb.
Amen Selah.

I rise at dawn, and there on high
Our dear Lord sits in the seventh sky.
Have pity on me, dear God, and on
My husband and my little ones.

Show me the way, a path that is good,
Your faithful hand will dole me food.
And what you dole will be my stay
Today and every day.

Dear my Lord, oh, come and be
Here inside this room with me,

גאט פון אברהם

גאט פון אברהם פון יצחק און' יעקב'ן
באהיט דיין ליבעס פאלק ישראל אין דיינעם לאב.

אז דער ליבע שבת קודש גייט אבעק
סמן טוב אז די גוטע וואך
וועט צו אונז קומען:
צו געזונט און' פרנסה צו לעבן, צו חן
אין חסד אין דין און' צו דת און' טהרת הלב
און' צו חזקת אברים צום אלען גוטען געוויין.
אמן סלה.

גאנץ פרי שטיי איך אויף
השם יתברך זיצט אין זיבעטן הימעל הויך.
ליבער גאט זוסט זיך דדברמען איבר מיר
איבר מיין מאן און' איבר מיינע קינדערלאך.

א גוטען שטעג און' וועג זוסטו מיר באווייזען
מיט דיין געטרייע האנד זוסטו מיך שפייזען
שפייזען זוסטו מיך מיט דיין גאב
היינט און' אלע טאג.

גאטעניו מיין
גיי אין מיין שטיב אריין

265

Bring with you sweet felicity.
Rule and bless the well, and heal
Those who sicken—let me feel
Free from human charity.

Elijah, the prophet, is in our house,
All evil things shall keep out,
All good shall enter by this door
And never leave us any more.

זאָסט מיר אַלע גוטע בשורות מבשר זיין.

די קראַנקע זאָסטו היילען

די געזונטע זאָסטו בענשען

מ׳זאָל ניט דערפען קא גאָב פון קא מענשען.

אליהו הנביא איז אין אונזער הויז

אלדעס בייז זאָל פון אונזער שטיב אַרויס

אלדעס גיטס זאָל אין אונזער שטיב אַריין

ס׳ זאָל ביי אונז אייביג זיין.

DAYS OF AWE

Grant Thy Awe

And so, O Lord our God, grant thy awe to all thy works,

and thy dread over all thou hast created,

that all thy works may fear thee,

and all who have been created prostrate themselves before thee,

and form one union

to do thy will with a whole heart.

For we know, O Lord our God,

that the kingdom is thine,

that power rests with thee,

that might is in thy right hand,

and that thy name is awesome over all thou hast created.

And so the righteous will see it and rejoice,

and the upright will jubilate,

and the devout break forth into songs of praise.

But violence will close her mouth,

and all wickedness vanish like smoke,

for thou shalt blot the rule of tyranny from the earth.

And thou alone shalt rule, O Lord, over thy works,

on the mountain of Zion, the seat of thy splendors,

and in Jerusalem, thy holy city,

as it is written in thy holy words:

"The Lord will reign for ever, thy God, O Zion, unto all gen-

    erations. Hallelujah."

תן פחדך

וּבְכֵן תֵּן פַּחְדְּךָ יְיָ אֱלֹהֵינוּ עַל כָּל מַעֲשֶׂיךָ

וְאֵימָתְךָ עַל כָּל מַה שֶׁבָּרָאתָ

וְיִירָאוּךָ כָּל הַמַּעֲשִׂים

וְיִשְׁתַּחֲווּ לְפָנֶיךָ כָּל הַבְּרוּאִים

וְיֵעָשׂוּ כֻלָּם אֲגֻדָּה אֶחָת

לַעֲשׂוֹת רְצוֹנְךָ בְּלֵבָב שָׁלֵם.

כְּמוֹ שֶׁיָּדַעְנוּ יְיָ אֱלֹהֵינוּ

שֶׁהַשִּׁלְטוֹן לְפָנֶיךָ

עֹז בְּיָדְךָ

וּגְבוּרָה בִּימִינֶךָ

וְשִׁמְךָ נוֹרָא עַל כָּל מַה שֶׁבָּרָאתָ.

וּבְכֵן צַדִּיקִים יִרְאוּ וְיִשְׂמָחוּ

וִישָׁרִים יַעֲלֹזוּ

וַחֲסִידִים בְּרִנָּה יָגִילוּ

וְעוֹלָתָה תִּקְפָּץ פִּיהָ

וְכָל הָרִשְׁעָה כֻּלָּהּ כְּעָשָׁן תִּכְלֶה

כִּי תַעֲבִיר מֶמְשֶׁלֶת זָדוֹן מִן הָאָרֶץ.

וְתִמְלוֹךְ אַתָּה יְיָ לְבַדֶּךָ עַל כָּל מַעֲשֶׂיךָ

בְּהַר צִיּוֹן מִשְׁכַּן כְּבוֹדֶךָ

וּבִירוּשָׁלַיִם עִיר קָדְשֶׁךָ

כַּכָּתוּב בְּדִבְרֵי קָדְשֶׁךָ

יִמְלֹךְ יְיָ לְעוֹלָם אֱלֹהַיִךְ צִיּוֹן לְדֹר וָדֹר הַלְלוּיָהּ.

It Is for Us to Praise

It is for us

to praise the Lord of all,

to sound the greatness of the Creator in the beginning,

who did not make us like the heathen of all lands,

nor set us like the families of earth,

who gave us a portion not like theirs,

a destiny unlike their multitudes.

And we bend the knee,

we bow before Him,

give our thanks

before the King over kings of kings,

the Holy One, blessed is He.

He spans the sky

and founds the earth,

the seat of His splendor

is heaven on high,

His power dwells

upon the summits.

He is our God,

there is no other.

True is our King.

Beside Him is naught.

עלינו

עָלֵינוּ

לְשַׁבֵּחַ לַאֲדוֹן הַכֹּל

לָתֵת גְּדֻלָּה לְיוֹצֵר בְּרֵאשִׁית

שֶׁלֹּא עָשָׂנוּ כְּגוֹיֵי הָאֲרָצוֹת

וְלֹא שָׂמָנוּ כְּמִשְׁפְּחוֹת הָאֲדָמָה

שֶׁלֹּא שָׂם חֶלְקֵנוּ כָּהֶם

וְגֹרָלֵנוּ כְּכָל הֲמוֹנָם.

וַאֲנַחְנוּ כֹּרְעִים

וּמִשְׁתַּחֲוִים

וּמוֹדִים

לִפְנֵי מֶלֶךְ מַלְכֵי הַמְּלָכִים

הַקָּדוֹשׁ בָּרוּךְ הוּא.

שֶׁהוּא נוֹטֶה שָׁמַיִם

וְיוֹסֵד אָרֶץ

וּמוֹשַׁב יְקָרוֹ

בַּשָּׁמַיִם מִמַּעַל

וּשְׁכִינַת עֻזּוֹ

בְּגָבְהֵי מְרוֹמִים

הוּא אֱלֹהֵינוּ

אֵין עוֹד.

אֱמֶת מַלְכֵּנוּ

אֶפֶס זוּלָתוֹ.

Therefore We Hope for Thee

Therefore, we hope for thee,
soon to see the splendor of thy strength,
O Lord our God,
when thou wilt cleanse the earth of every idol
and strike their statues down,
that the world may find perfection under the kingdom of the
    Almighty,
that all the sons of flesh call out thy name,
all the wicked of the earth turn unto thee.

All dwellers in the world will see and know
that every knee is bowed to thee
and every tongue avows thee.
Before thee, O Lord our God, they will kneel and fall
to give honor to the glory of thy name.
And all will take upon themselves
the yoke of thy kingdom,
and thou, King over them
soon, forever and ever.

For the kingdom is thine,
for endless ages thou shalt be King in glory.

המלכות שלך היא

עַל כֵּן נְקַוֶּה לְךָ
יְיָ אֱלֹהֵינוּ
לִרְאוֹת מְהֵרָה בְּתִפְאֶרֶת עֻזֶּךָ
לְהַעֲבִיר גִּלּוּלִים מִן הָאָרֶץ
וְהָאֱלִילִים כָּרוֹת יִכָּרֵתוּן
לְתַקֵּן עוֹלָם בְּמַלְכוּת שַׁדַּי
וְכָל בְּנֵי בָשָׂר יִקְרְאוּ בִשְׁמֶךָ
לְהַפְנוֹת אֵלֶיךָ כָּל רִשְׁעֵי אָרֶץ.

יַכִּירוּ וְיֵדְעוּ כָּל יוֹשְׁבֵי תֵבֵל
כִּי לְךָ תִּכְרַע כָּל בֶּרֶךְ
תִּשָּׁבַע כָּל לָשׁוֹן.
לְפָנֶיךָ יְיָ אֱלֹהֵינוּ יִכְרְעוּ וְיִפּוֹלוּ
וְלִכְבוֹד שִׁמְךָ יְקָר יִתֵּנוּ
וִיקַבְּלוּ כֻלָּם
אֶת עֹל מַלְכוּתֶךָ
וְתִמְלוֹךְ עֲלֵיהֶם
מְהֵרָה לְעוֹלָם וָעֶד.

כִּי הַמַּלְכוּת שֶׁלְּךָ הִיא
וּלְעוֹלְמֵי עַד תִּמְלוֹךְ בְּכָבוֹד.

Reign over All the Universe

Our God and God of our fathers,

reign over all the universe in thine honor,

and be upborne above all the earth in thy glory,

and appear in the glorious pride of thy power

over all that inhabit this globe, thine earth.

Let every made thing know thou made it,

and every form comprehend thou formed it,

and let each say that has breath in his lungs,

the Lord God of Israel is King,

and His kingdom is in all.

Sanctify us in thy commandments,

and give us a share in thy Torah;

sate us with thy bounty,

and rejoice us in thy salvation,

and purify our hearts to serve thee truthfully.

For thou art a God of truth

and thy word is truth

and enduring forever.

מלוך על כל העולם

אֱלֹהֵינוּ וֵאלֹהֵי אֲבוֹתֵינוּ
מְלוֹךְ עַל כָּל הָעוֹלָם כֻּלּוֹ בִּכְבוֹדֶךָ
וְהִנָּשֵׂא עַל כָּל הָאָרֶץ בִּיקָרֶךָ
וְהוֹפַע בַּהֲדַר גְּאוֹן עֻזֶּךָ
עַל כָּל יוֹשְׁבֵי תֵבֵל אַרְצֶךָ.

וְיֵדַע כָּל פָּעוּל כִּי אַתָּה פְעַלְתּוֹ
וְיָבִין כָּל יָצוּר כִּי אַתָּה יְצַרְתּוֹ
וְיֹאמַר כֹּל אֲשֶׁר נְשָׁמָה בְּאַפּוֹ
יְיָ אֱלֹהֵי יִשְׂרָאֵל מֶלֶךְ
וּמַלְכוּתוֹ בַּכֹּל מָשָׁלָה.

קַדְּשֵׁנוּ בְּמִצְוֹתֶיךָ
וְתֵן חֶלְקֵנוּ בְּתוֹרָתֶךָ
שַׂבְּעֵנוּ מִטּוּבֶךָ
וְשַׂמְּחֵנוּ בִּישׁוּעָתֶךָ
וְטַהֵר לִבֵּנוּ לְעָבְדְּךָ בֶּאֱמֶת.

כִּי אַתָּה אֱלֹהִים אֱמֶת
וּדְבָרְךָ אֱמֶת
וְקַיָּם לָעַד.

Remembrance

Thou dost remember how the world was made,

thou dost keep in mind all those formed of old;

before thee all hid things are bare,

the throng of secrets from of yore.

For there is no forgetting

before thy throne of honor

and nothing secret from thine eyes.

Thou dost remember all that was done

and no form is concealed from thee.

All is bared and known before thee,

O Lord our God,

thou art he who looks and sees

to the end of all generations.

From the first thou hast let it be known,

and from of yore this thou hast bared:

that thou shalt bring memorial tide

to remember all the souls and spirits,

to bethink thee of many deeds,

and of thy creatures, the endless throng.

זכרונות

אַתָּה זוֹכֵר מַעֲשֵׂה עוֹלָם

וּפוֹקֵד כָּל יְצוּרֵי קֶדֶם

לְפָנֶיךָ נִגְלוּ כָּל תַּעֲלוּמוֹת

וַהֲמוֹן נִסְתָּרוֹת שֶׁמִּבְּרֵאשִׁית.

אֵין שִׁכְחָה

לִפְנֵי כִסֵּא כְבוֹדֶךָ

וְאֵין נִסְתָּר מִנֶּגֶד עֵינֶיךָ.

אַתָּה זוֹכֵר אֶת כָּל הַמִּפְעָל

וְגַם כָּל הַיְצוּר לֹא נִכְחַד מִמֶּךָּ.

הַכֹּל גָּלוּי וְיָדוּעַ לְפָנֶיךָ

יְיָ אֱלֹהֵינוּ

צוֹפֶה וּמַבִּיט

עַד סוֹף כָּל הַדּוֹרוֹת.

כִּי תָבִיא חֹק זִכָּרוֹן

לְהִפָּקֵד כָּל רוּחַ וָנָפֶשׁ

לְהִזָּכֵר מַעֲשִׂים רַבִּים

וַהֲמוֹן בְּרִיּוֹת לְאֵין תַּכְלִית

מֵרֵאשִׁית כָּזֹאת הוֹדָעְתָּ

וּמִלְּפָנִים אוֹתָהּ גִּלִּיתָ.

Before I Was Formed

My God,

before I was formed

I was worth nothing,

and now that I am formed,

it is as though I had not been formed.

Dust I am in life,

and how much more in death.

Here am I, in thy presence,

like a vessel filled with shame and disgrace.

Be it thy will, O Lord my God,

that I sin no more.

And the sins I have committed in thy presence,

wipe them away in thy great mercy,

but not with suffering and grave sickness.

עד שלא נוצרתי

אֱלֹהַי
עַד שֶׁלֹּא נוֹצַרְתִּי
אֵינִי כְדַי
וְעַכְשָׁו שֶׁנּוֹצַרְתִּי
כְּאִלּוּ לֹא נוֹצַרְתִּי.
עָפָר אֲנִי בְּחַיַּי
קַל וָחֹמֶר בְּמִיתָתִי.

הֲרֵי אֲנִי לְפָנֶיךָ
כִּכְלִי מָלֵא בוּשָׁה וּכְלִמָּה.

יְהִי רָצוֹן מִלְּפָנֶיךָ יְיָ אֱלֹהַי
שֶׁלֹּא אֶחֱטָא עוֹד
וּמַה שֶּׁחָטָאתִי לְפָנֶיךָ
מָרֵק בְּרַחֲמֶיךָ הָרַבִּים
אֲבָל לֹא עַל יְדֵי יִסּוּרִים וָחֳלָיִם רָעִים.

Our God Who Art in Heaven

Our God who art in heaven, reveal the glory of thy kingdom
    unto us speedily.

Our God who art in heaven, we have earnestly sought thee,
    grant that we may find thee.

Our God who art in heaven, command thy blessings to be
    with us.

Our God who art in heaven, command thy salvation to be
    with us.

Our God who art in heaven, hasten for us the appointed re-
    demption.

Our God who art in heaven, draw us near to thy service.

Our God who art in heaven, grant peace to reign in our midst.

Our God who art in heaven, give life and peace to our sover-
    eign lord the King.

Our God who art in heaven, grant peace to the earth.

Our God who art in heaven, bestow plenty on thy world.

אלהינו שבשמים

אֱלֹהֵינוּ שֶׁבַּשָּׁמַיִם גַּלֵּה כְּבוֹד מַלְכוּתְךָ עָלֵינוּ מְהֵרָה.

אֱלֹהֵינוּ שֶׁבַּשָּׁמַיִם דְּרַשְׁנוּךָ הִמָּצֵא־לָנוּ.

אֱלֹהֵינוּ שֶׁבַּשָּׁמַיִם צַוֵּה אִתָּנוּ בְּרְכוֹתֶיךָ.

אֱלֹהֵינוּ שֶׁבַּשָּׁמַיִם צַוֵּה אִתָּנוּ יְשׁוּעוֹתֶיךָ.

אֱלֹהֵינוּ שֶׁבַּשָּׁמַיִם קָרֵב לָנוּ קֵץ הַגְּאֻלָּה.

אֱלֹהֵינוּ שֶׁבַּשָּׁמַיִם קָרְבֵנוּ לַעֲבֹדָתֶיךָ.

אֱלֹהֵינוּ שֶׁבַּשָּׁמַיִם שִׁית שָׁלוֹם בֵּינֵינוּ.

אֱלֹהֵינוּ שֶׁבַּשָּׁמַיִם תֵּן חַיִּים וְשָׁלוֹם לַמֶּלֶךְ אֲדוֹנֵינוּ.

אֱלֹהֵינוּ שֶׁבַּשָּׁמַיִם תֵּן שָׁלוֹם בָּאָרֶץ.

אֱלֹהֵינוּ שֶׁבַּשָּׁמַיִם תֵּן שָׂבָע בְּעוֹלָמֶךָ.

I Shall Flee from Thee to Thee

O my God, if my sin is too great to bear,

what wilt thou do for thy great name?

If I cannot hope for thy mercies,

who but thou will have pity on me?

Therefore, though thou kill me, I shall hope in thee,

and if thou search out my sin, I shall flee from thee to thee,

and hide myself from thy wrath in thy shadow.

I shall hold on to the skirts of thy mercy until thou hast pity on

me.

"I will not let thee go, except thou bless me."

Give me new life,

and from the depths of the earth raise me up again,

and I shall say: "I praise thee, Lord, for though thou wert

angry with me, thou didst soften thine anger and pity me."

Thine is the mercy, O God, in all the good which thou hast

vouchsafed to me

and which thou wilt vouchsafe to me until the day I die.

אברח ממך אליך

אֱלֹהַי אִם עֲוֹנִי מִנְּשׂוֹא גָּדוֹל
מַה תַּעֲשֶׂה לְשִׁמְךָ הַגָּדוֹל.
וְאִם לֹא אוֹחִיל לְרַחֲמֶיךָ
מִי יָחוּס עָלַי חוּץ מִמֶּךָּ.
לָכֵן אִם תִּקְטְלֵנִי לְךָ אֲיַחֵל
וְאִם תְּבַקֵּשׁ לַעֲוֹנִי אֶבְרַח מִמְּךָ אֵלֶיךָ
וְאֶתְכַּסֶּה מֵחֲמָתְךָ בְּצִלֶּךָ.
וּבְשׁוּלֵי רַחֲמֶיךָ אַחֲזִיק עַד אִם רִחַמְתָּנִי
וְלֹא אֲשַׁלֵּחֲךָ כִּי אִם בֵּרַכְתָּנִי.

וְתָשׁוּב תְּחַיֵּנִי
וּמִתְּהֹמֹת הָאָרֶץ תָּשׁוּב תַּעֲלֵנִי
וְאֹמַר אוֹדְךָ יְיָ כִּי אָנַפְתָּ בִּי יָשׁוּב אַפְּךָ וּתְנַחֲמֵנִי.
וּלְךָ יְיָ חֶסֶד עַל כָּל הַטּוֹבָה אֲשֶׁר גְּמַלְתָּנִי
וַאֲשֶׁר עַד יוֹם מוֹתִי תִּגְמְלֵנִי.

The Reader's Prayer

Here am I, poor in deeds,

trembling and frightened, in fear of Him who dwells amid the

praises of Israel.

I have come to stand before thee and plead for Israel, thy people,

who have sent me,

though I am neither fit nor worthy for it.

Yet do I ask of thee,

God of Abraham, God of Isaac, and God of Jacob,

O Lord, merciful and gracious, God of Israel,

almighty, tremendous and awesome:

Help me succeed as I stand and seek compassion for myself and

for those who have sent me.

O condemn them not for my sins,

do not account them guilty for my iniquities,

for I am a sinner and a transgressor.

O suffer them not to be confounded for my transgressions,

let them not be ashamed of me,

and let me not be ashamed of them.

Let our banner be love;

cover our transgressions in love.

Our fasts and afflictions turn for us and all Israel

into joy and gladness,

תְּפִלָּה לִשְׁלִיחַ צִבּוּר

הִנְנִי הֶעָנִי מִמַּעַשׂ
נִרְעַשׁ וְנִפְחָד
מִפַּחַד יוֹשֵׁב תְּהִלּוֹת יִשְׂרָאֵל.
בָּאתִי לַעֲמֹד וּלְהִתְחַנֵּן לְפָנֶיךָ
עַל עַמְּךָ יִשְׂרָאֵל אֲשֶׁר שְׁלָחוּנִי
אַף עַל פִּי שֶׁאֵינִי כְדַי וְהָגוּן לְכָךְ.
לָכֵן אֲבַקֵּשׁ מִמְּךָ
אֱלֹהֵי אַבְרָהָם אֱלֹהֵי יִצְחָק וֵאלֹהֵי יַעֲקֹב
יְיָ יְיָ אֵל רַחוּם וְחַנּוּן אֱלֹהֵי יִשְׂרָאֵל
שַׁדַּי אָיֹם וְנוֹרָא
הֱיֵה נָא מַצְלִיחַ דַּרְכִּי אֲשֶׁר אֲנִי הוֹלֵךְ
לַעֲמֹד וּלְבַקֵּשׁ רַחֲמִים עָלַי וְעַל שׁוֹלְחָי.

נָא אַל תַּפְשִׁיעֵם בְּחַטֹּאתִי
וְאַל תְּחַיְּבֵם בַּעֲוֹנוֹתַי
כִּי חוֹטֵא וּפוֹשֵׁעַ אָנִי.
וְאַל יִכָּלְמוּ בִּפְשָׁעַי
וְאַל יֵבוֹשׁוּ הֵם בִּי
וְאַל אֵבוֹשׁ אֲנִי בָּהֶם.

וִיהִי נָא דִגְלֵנוּ עָלֶיךָ אַהֲבָה
וְעַל כָּל פְּשָׁעִים תְּכַסֶּה בְּאַהֲבָה.
כָּל צָרוֹת וְרָעוֹת הֲפָךְ־נָא לָנוּ וּלְכָל יִשְׂרָאֵל
לְשָׂשׂוֹן וּלְשִׂמְחָה

into life and peace.

"Truth and peace shall ye love."

O may there be no stumbling in my prayer.

לְחַיִּים וּלְשָׁלוֹם.
הָאֱמֶת וְהַשָּׁלוֹם אֱהָבוּ
וְלֹא יְהִי שׁוּם מִכְשׁוֹל בִּתְפִלָּתִי.

Thou Givest a Hand to Transgressors

Thou givest a hand to transgressors,

thy right hand is ever open to receive the repentant.

Thou hast taught us, O Lord our God,

to confess our sins before thee,

to cease committing wrong,

that we may be accepted into thy presence in perfect repentance.

Thou hast distinguished man from the very beginning,

and hast deemed him worthy to stand before thee;

for who shall say unto thee, what doest thou?

And if man be righteous, can he benefit thee?

But thou in thy love hast given us, O Lord our God,

this Day of Atonement

for pardon and forgiveness.

Have mercy upon us,

for thou delightest not in the destruction of the world,

as it is said:

"Seek the Lord, while he may be found,

call upon him while he is near."

אַתָּה נוֹתֵן יָד לְפוֹשְׁעִים

אַתָּה נוֹתֵן יָד לְפוֹשְׁעִים
וִימִינְךָ פְּשׁוּטָה לְקַבֵּל שָׁבִים.
וַתְּלַמְּדֵנוּ יְיָ אֱלֹהֵינוּ
לְהִתְוַדּוֹת לְפָנֶיךָ עַל כָּל־עֲווֹנוֹתֵינוּ
לְמַעַן נֶחְדַּל מֵעֹשֶׁק יָדֵינוּ
וּתְקַבְּלֵנוּ בִּתְשׁוּבָה שְׁלֵמָה לְפָנֶיךָ.

אַתָּה הִבְדַּלְתָּ אֱנוֹשׁ מֵרֹאשׁ
וַתַּכִּירֵהוּ לַעֲמוֹד לְפָנֶיךָ
כִּי מִי יֹאמַר לְךָ מַה־תִּפְעַל
וְאִם־יִצְדַּק מַה־יִּתֶּן־לָךְ.
וַתִּתֶּן לָנוּ יְיָ אֱלֹהֵינוּ בְּאַהֲבָה
אֶת יוֹם הַכִּפֻּרִים הַזֶּה
קֵץ וּמְחִילָה וּסְלִיחָה.
רַחֵם עָלֵינוּ
כִּי לֹא תַחְפֹּץ בְּהַשְׁחָתַת עוֹלָם
שֶׁנֶּאֱמַר
דִּרְשׁוּ יְיָ בְּהִמָּצְאוֹ
קְרָאֻהוּ בִּהְיוֹתוֹ קָרוֹב.

The Dwellers on High

The dwellers on high and the dwellers below,

they fear, they shudder in dread of your name;

the dwellers in the deep and the dwellers among the shades,

they quake, they tremble in dread of your verdict;

but the just in the Garden of Eden—

they sing and they chant to your name.

Therefore, I, Levi Yitzhak, son of Sarah,

have come before you in prayer and plea.

What have you to do with Israel?

"Command." But whom do you command?

The children of Israel.

"So shall you bless..." But whom do you bid to bless?

The children of Israel.

Therefore, I ask you: What have you to do with Israel?

Are there not many peoples: Chaldeans, Persians, Ishmaelites,
    and Midianites?

What have you to do with Israel?

Hence it must be that Israel is dear to you, for they are called
    the sons of God.

"Blessed are you, O Lord our God...."

דרי מעלה

דרי מעלה עם דרי מטה
יפחדון וירעדון מאימת שמך.
דרי תהום עם דרי שאול
ירעשון וירגזון מאימת דינך.
אבל צדיקים ממקום גן עדן
ירננו ויזמרו לשמך.
לכן אני לוי יצחק בן שרה
באתי לפניך בתפילתי ובבקשתי.
מה לך אצל ישראל.
צו. את מי תצוה.
את בני ישראל.
כה תברכו. את מי אתה מצוה לברך.
את בני ישראל.
לכן אני שואל אותך מה לך אצל ישראל.
הלא יש כמה אומות כשדים פרסיים ישמעאלים מדיינים.
מה לך אצל ישראל.
אלא מכאן מוכח חביבין ישראל שנקראו בנים למקום.
ברוך אתה יי׳ אלהינו . . .

Illumine My Eyes

Take away my shame, lift my disquiet,
annul my sin
that I may pray before thee with gladness of heart,
to turn to thy commandments and thy law
in the joy of holiness.
Grant me to bring joy to all thy creatures,
to lift up and make noble those who fear thee,
to give much goodness, mercy and blessing in the world.
Humble the arrogant
who have tried to pervert me with falsehood,
while I sought my happiness in serving thee.
Save me from weakness, from faltering
and from every evil trait,
illumine my eyes with the light of thy deliverance.
Help thy people,
imbue the heart of thy people with reverence
and with awe before thy majesty.
Strengthen them with thy love,
guide them to walk in the path of thy righteousness,
kindle in their hearts
the gracious light of this your holy Sabbath
and bring them to possess the inheritance
thou hast set for them,
soon, soon, near to these our days.

הַעֲבֵר חֶרְפָּתִי הָסֵר דַּאֲגָתִי

מְחֵה פְּשָׁעַי

כְּדֵי שֶׁאוּכַל לְהִתְפַּלֵּל לְפָנֶיךָ בִּמְאוֹר פָּנִים

לַעֲסוֹק בְּמִצְוֹתֶיךָ וּבְתוֹרָתֶךָ

בְּשִׂמְחַת קֹדֶשׁ.

אֶזְכֶּה נָא לְשַׂמֵּחַ אֶת־בְּרִיּוֹתֶיךָ

לְרוֹמֵם וּלְפָאֵר אֶת־יְרֵאֶיךָ.

זַכֵּנִי לְהַרְבּוֹת טוֹבָה וָחֶסֶד וּבְרָכָה בָּעוֹלָם.

יֵבשׁוּ זֵדִים

כִּי שֶׁקֶר עִוְּתוּנִי

וַאֲנִי בְּפִקּוּדֶיךָ אֶשְׁתַּעֲשָׁע.

הַצִּילֵנִי מִכָּל־חֻלְשָׁה מִכָּל־רִפְיוֹן

וּמִכָּל־מִדָּה רָעָה.

הָאִירָה עֵינַי בְּהֶאָרַת שְׂשׂוֹן יִשְׁעֶךָ.

הוֹשִׁיעָה אֶת־עַמֶּךָ

תֵּן בְּלֵב עַם קָדְשֶׁךָ יִרְאָתֶךָ

וּפַחַד הֲדַר גְּאוֹן עֻזֶּךָ.

סָמְכֵם בְּאַהֲבָתֶךָ

יַשְּׁרֵם נָא בְּיֹשֶׁר מְסִלָּתֶךָ.

הוֹפַע בְּלִבָּם

הֶאָרַת חֶמְדַּת נְעִימַת קְדֻשַׁת שַׁבַּת קָדְשֶׁךָ

וַהֲשִׁיבֵם אֶל נַחֲלָתֶךָ

בִּמְהֵרָה בִּמְהֵרָה בְּיָמֵינוּ בְּקָרוֹב.

Open unto Us the Gate

Open unto us the gate
at the time of closing the gate,
now that the day is turning.

The day is turning,
the sun is setting and turning.
O let us enter in thy gate.

פתח לנו שער

פְּתַח לָנוּ שַׁעַר
בְּעֵת נְעִילַת שַׁעַר
כִּי פָנָה יוֹם.

הַיּוֹם יִפְנֶה
הַשֶּׁמֶשׁ יָבֹא וְיִפְנֶה
נָבוֹאָה שְׁעָרֶיךָ.

The Closing of the Gate

God, tremendous for thy doings,
send forgiveness to us
in the hour of closing.

Those once-called the remnant
tremble, shuddering,
they lift their eyes to thee,
in the hour of closing.

They pour their hearts to thee;
erase their sin and their denying,
send to them forgiveness
in the hour of closing.

Be their covering,
save them from scourging,
seal them unto joy,
in the hour of closing.

Open heaven's gates
to hearts as water pouring,
announce to them—redemption
in the hour of closing.

בשעת הנעילה

אֵל נוֹרָא עֲלִילָה
הַמְצִיא לָנוּ מְחִילָה
בִּשְׁעַת הַנְּעִילָה.

מְתֵי מִסְפָּר קְרוּאִים
לְךָ עַיִן נוֹשְׂאִים
וּמְסַלְדִים בְּחִילָה
בִּשְׁעַת הַנְּעִילָה.

שׁוֹפְכִים לְךָ נַפְשָׁם
מְחֵה פִּשְׁעָם וְכַחֲשָׁם
וְהַמְצִיאֵם מְחִילָה
בִּשְׁעַת הַנְּעִילָה.

הֱיֵה לָהֶם לְסִתְרָה
וְחַלְּצֵם מִמְּאֵרָה
וְחָתְמֵם נָא לְגִילָה
בִּשְׁעַת הַנְּעִילָה.

פְּתַח שַׁעֲרֵי שָׁמַיִם
לְשׁוֹפְכִים לֵב כַּמַּיִם
וּבַשְּׂרֵם נָא הַגְּאֻלָּה
בִּשְׁעַת הַנְּעִילָה.

PEACE

Set Peace, Goodness and Blessing

Set peace, goodness and blessing,
grace and mercy and compassion,
on us and all Israel, thy folk.

Bless us, our Father,
one and all,
in the light of thy countenance.

For in that light
hast thou given us,
O Lord our God,
living Torah,
and merciful love,
righteousness, blessing,
compassion and life and peace.

And let it be good in thine eyes
to bless thy folk Israel,
at every time and at every hour
with thy peace.

שים שלום

שִׂים שָׁלוֹם טוֹבָה וּבְרָכָה
חֵן וָחֶסֶד וְרַחֲמִים
עָלֵינוּ וְעַל כָּל יִשְׂרָאֵל עַמֶּךָ.

בָּרְכֵנוּ אָבִינוּ
כֻּלָּנוּ כְּאֶחָד
בְּאוֹר פָּנֶיךָ.

כִּי בְאוֹר פָּנֶיךָ
נָתַתָּ לָּנוּ
יְיָ אֱלֹהֵינוּ
תּוֹרַת חַיִּים
וְאַהֲבַת חֶסֶד
וּצְדָקָה וּבְרָכָה
וְרַחֲמִים וְחַיִּים וְשָׁלוֹם.

וְטוֹב בְּעֵינֶיךָ
לְבָרֵךְ אֶת עַמְּךָ יִשְׂרָאֵל
בְּכָל עֵת וּבְכָל שָׁעָה
בִּשְׁלוֹמֶךָ.

Walk Me in Peace

Be it thy will, O Lord my God,

that thou walk me in peace, direct my steps in peace,

and support me in peace.

Save me from the hand of every foe, and every ambush on my

    way.

Send a blessing on the works of my hands,

and give me grace, favor, and compassion in thine eyes,

and in the eyes of all who see me.

תוֹלִיכֵנִי לשלום

יְהִי רָצוֹן מִלְּפָנֶיךָ יְיָ אֱלֹהַי
שֶׁתּוֹלִיכֵנִי לְשָׁלוֹם וְתַצְעִידֵנִי לְשָׁלוֹם
וְתִסְמְכֵנִי לְשָׁלוֹם
וְתַצִּילֵנִי מִכַּף כָּל אוֹיֵב וְאוֹרֵב בַּדָּרֶךְ.

וְתִשְׁלַח בְּרָכָה בְּמַעֲשֵׂה יָדַי
וְתִתְּנֵנִי לְחֵן וּלְחֶסֶד וּלְרַחֲמִים בְּעֵינֶיךָ
וּבְעֵינֵי כָל רוֹאָי.

Love and Brotherliness

Be it thy will, O Lord our God,

to cause to dwell in our lot, love, brotherliness, peace, and
    friendship;

to widen our boundaries through disciples,

to prosper our goal with hope and with future,

to appoint us a share in the Garden of Eden,

to direct us in thy world through good companions and good
    impulse,

that we may rise in the morning and find

our heart waiting to fear thy name.

אַהֲבָה וְאַחֲוָה

יְהִי רָצוֹן מִלְּפָנֶיךָ יְיָ אֱלֹהֵינוּ
שֶׁתַּשְׁכֵּן בְּפוּרֵנוּ אַהֲבָה וְאַחֲוָה וְשָׁלוֹם וְרֵעוּת
וְתַרְבֶּה גְבוּלֵנוּ בְּתַלְמִידִים
וְתַצְלִיחַ סוֹפֵנוּ אַחֲרִית וְתִקְוָה
וְתָשִׂים חֶלְקֵנוּ בְּגַן עֵדֶן
וְתַקְּנֵנוּ בְּחָבֵר טוֹב וְיֵצֶר טוֹב בְּעוֹלָמֶךָ

וְנִשְׂכִּים וְנִמְצָא יִחוּל לְבָבֵנוּ
לְיִרְאָה אֶת שְׁמֶךָ.

Keep My Tongue from Evil

My God,

Keep my tongue from evil,

and my lips from speaking guile.

To those who curse me, let my soul be silent,

my soul shall be to all as dust.

Open my heart to thy law,

let my soul hasten to do thy commandments.

Be the words of my mouth and my heart's meditation

acceptable in thy presence,

O Lord, my Rock and my Redeemer.

נְצוֹר לְשׁוֹנִי מֵרָע

אֱלֹהַי

נְצוֹר לְשׁוֹנִי מֵרָע

וּשְׂפָתַי מִדַּבֵּר מִרְמָה

וְלִמְקַלְלַי נַפְשִׁי תִדּוֹם

וְנַפְשִׁי כֶּעָפָר לַכֹּל תִּהְיֶה.

פְּתַח לִבִּי בְּתוֹרָתֶךָ

וּבְמִצְוֹתֶיךָ תִּרְדּוֹף נַפְשִׁי.

יִהְיוּ לְרָצוֹן אִמְרֵי פִי

וְהֶגְיוֹן לִבִּי לְפָנֶיךָ

יְיָ צוּרִי וְגוֹאֲלִי.

No Hatred

May this be your will, O Lord my God and God of my fathers:

that hatred for us overcome no man,

and hatred for no man overcome us;

that jealousy of us overcome no man,

and jealousy of no man overcome us;

that your Torah be our lifelong vocation,

and our words supplications before you.

אל תשנא

יְהִי רָצוֹן מִלְּפָנֶיךָ יְיָ אֱלֹהַי וֵאלֹהֵי אֲבוֹתַי
שֶׁלֹּא תַעֲלֶה שִׂנְאָתֵנוּ עַל לֵב אָדָם
וְלֹא שִׂנְאַת אָדָם תַּעֲלֶה עַל לִבֵּנוּ.
וְלֹא תַעֲלֶה קִנְאָתֵנוּ עַל לֵב אָדָם
וְלֹא קִנְאַת אָדָם תַּעֲלֶה עַל לִבֵּנוּ.
וּתְהֵא תוֹרָתְךָ מְלַאכְתֵּנוּ כָּל יְמֵי חַיֵּינוּ
וְיִהְיוּ דְּבָרֵינוּ תַּחֲנוּנִים לְפָנֶיךָ.

Lord of Peace

O Lord and King of peace,

who makes peace and creates all things:

Help all of us, that we may forever adhere to the concept of
   peace,

so that true and abundant peace prevail between man and
   man, between husband and wife,

and no strife separate mankind even in thought.

You make peace in your heavens, you bring contrary elements
   harmoniously together:

Extend abundant peace to us and to the whole world,

so that all discords be resolved in great love and peace,

and with one mind and one heart all come near to you and
   your law in truth,

and all form one union to do your will with a whole heart.

O Lord of peace, bless us with peace.

אֲדוֹן הַשָּׁלוֹם

אֲדוֹן הַשָּׁלוֹם מֶלֶךְ שֶׁהַשָּׁלוֹם שֶׁלּוֹ
עוֹשֶׂה שָׁלוֹם וּבוֹרֵא אֶת הַכֹּל
עָזְרֵנוּ וְהוֹשִׁיעֵנוּ כֻּלָּנוּ שֶׁנִּזְכֶּה תָמִיד לֶאֱחוֹז בְּמִדַּת הַשָּׁלוֹם
וְיִהְיֶה שָׁלוֹם גָּדוֹל בֶּאֱמֶת בֵּין כָּל אָדָם לַחֲבֵרוֹ וּבֵין אִישׁ וְאִשְׁתּוֹ
וְלֹא יִהְיֶה שׁוּם מַחֲלוֹקֶת אֲפִילוּ בַלֵּב בֵּין כָּל בְּנֵי אָדָם.
אַתָּה עוֹשֶׂה שָׁלוֹם בִּמְרוֹמֶיךָ וְאַתָּה מְחַבֵּר שְׁנֵי הַפָכִים יַחַד אֵשׁ
וּמַיִם וּבְנִפְלְאוֹתֶיךָ הָעֲצוּמִים אַתָּה עוֹשֶׂה שָׁלוֹם בֵּינֵיהֶם
כֵּן תַּמְשִׁיךְ שָׁלוֹם גָּדוֹל עָלֵינוּ וְעַל כָּל הָעוֹלָם כֻּלּוֹ
בְּאוֹפֶן שֶׁיִּתְחַבְּרוּ כָּל הַהֲפָכִים יַחַד בְּשָׁלוֹם גָּדוֹל וּבְאַהֲבָה גְדוֹלָה
וְיִכָּלְלוּ כֻלָּם בְּדֵעָה אַחַת וְלֵב אֶחָד לְהִתְקָרֵב אֵלֶיךָ וּלְתוֹרָתְךָ
בֶּאֱמֶת
וְיֵעָשׂוּ כֻלָּם אֲגוּדָה אַחַת לַעֲשׂוֹת רְצוֹנְךָ בְּלֵבָב שָׁלֵם.
יְיָ שָׁלוֹם בָּרְכֵנוּ בְשָׁלוֹם.

Annul Wars and the Shedding of Blood

Be it thy will

to annul wars and the shedding of blood from the universe,

and to extend a peace, great and wondrous, in the universe.

"Nor again shall one people raise the sword against another

and they shall learn war no more."

But let all the residents of earth recognize and know the inner-

    most truth:

that we are not come into this world for quarrel and division,

nor for hate and jealousy, contrariness and bloodshed;

but we are come into this world

thee to recognize and know,

be thou blessed forever.

And let thy glory fill all our wits and minds, knowledge and

    hearts;

and may I be a chariot for the presence of thy divinity.

May I not again depart from the Sanctity as much as a hairs-

    breadth.

May I not think one extraneous thought.

But may I ever cling to thee and to thy sacred Torah,

until I be worthy to introduce others into the knowledge of the

    truth of thy divinity.

"To announce to the sons of man thy power,

and the honor of the glory of thy kingdom."

לא ילמדו עוד מלחמה

יְהִי רָצוֹן מִלְּפָנֶיךָ
שֶׁתְּבַטֵּל מִלְחָמוֹת וּשְׁפִיכוּת דָּמִים מִן הָעוֹלָם
וְתַמְשִׁיךְ שָׁלוֹם גָּדוֹל וְנִפְלָא בָּעוֹלָם.
וְלֹא יִשְׂאוּ עוֹד גּוֹי אֶל גּוֹי חֶרֶב
וְלֹא יִלְמְדוּ עוֹד מִלְחָמָה.

רַק יַכִּירוּ וְיֵדְעוּ כָּל יוֹשְׁבֵי תֵבֵל הָאֱמֶת לַאֲמִתּוֹ
אֲשֶׁר לֹא בָאנוּ לָזֶה הָעוֹלָם בִּשְׁבִיל רִיב וּמַחֲלוֹקֶת
וְלֹא בִּשְׁבִיל שִׂנְאָה וְקִנְאָה וְקִנְתּוּר וּשְׁפִיכוּת דָּמִים
רַק בָּאנוּ לָעוֹלָם
כְּדֵי לְהַכִּיר וְלָדַעַת אוֹתְךָ
תִּתְבָּרַךְ לָנֶצַח.

וִימַלֵּא כְבוֹדְךָ אֶת כָּל מוֹחֵנוּ וְשִׂכְלֵנוּ וְדַעְתֵּנוּ וּלְבָבֵנוּ
וְאֶהְיֶה מֶרְכָּבָה לִשְׁכִינַת אֱלֹהוּתֶךָ.
וְלֹא אֵצֵא עוֹד מִן הַקְּדֻשָּׁה אֲפִילוּ כְחוּט הַשַּׂעֲרָה
וְלֹא אֶחְשׁוֹב שׁוּם מַחֲשֶׁבֶת חוּץ.
רַק אֶהְיֶה תָמִיד דָּבוּק בְּךָ וּבְתוֹרָתְךָ הַקְּדוֹשָׁה
עַד שֶׁאֶזְכֶּה לְהַכְנִיס גַּם בַּאֲחֵרִים יְדִיעַת אֲמִתַּת אֱלֹהוּתֶךָ.
לְהוֹדִיעַ לִבְנֵי הָאָדָם גְּבוּרָתְךָ
וּכְבוֹד הֲדַר מַלְכוּתֶךָ.

Guard Us from Vicious Leanings

Guard us
from vicious leanings and from haughty ways,
from anger and from temper,
from melancholy, talebearing,
and from all the other evil qualities.

Nor let envy of any man rise in our heart,
nor envy of us in the heart of others.

On the contrary:
put it in our hearts that we may see our comrades' virtue,
and not their failing.

תשמרנו מן הפניות

תִּשְׁמְרֵנוּ

מִן הַפְּנִיּוֹת וְהַגַּאֲווֹת

וּמִן הַכַּעַס וְהַקַּפְּדָנוּת

וְהָעַצְבוּת וְהָרְכִילוּת

וּשְׁאָר מִדּוֹת רָעוֹת.

וְלֹא תַעֲלֶה קִנְאַת אָדָם עַל לִבֵּנוּ

וְלֹא קִנְאָתֵנוּ עַל אֲחֵרִים

אַדְרַבָּה

תֵּן בְּלִבֵּנוּ שֶׁנִּרְאֶה כָּל אֶחָד מַעֲלַת חֲבֵרֵינוּ

וְלֹא חֶסְרוֹנָם.

May He Bless Thee

MAY HE BLESS THEE with all good

AND KEEP THEE from all evil.

MAY HE ENLIGHTEN thy heart with immortal wisdom

AND GRACE THEE with eternal knowledge.

MAY HE LIFT UP HIS merciful COUNTENANCE UPON THEE

for eternal peace.

יברככה

יְבָרֶכְכָה בְּכוֹל טוֹב
וְיִשְׁמוֹרְכָה מִכּוֹל רָע
וְיָאִיר לִבְּכָה בְּשֵׂכֶל חַיִּים
וְיָחוֹנְכָה בְּדַעַת עוֹלָמִים
וְיִשָּׂא פְּנֵי חֲסָדָיו לְכָה
לִשְׁלוֹם עוֹלָמִים.

NOTES AND

ACKNOWLEDGMENTS

40 YOU ARE HE WHO WAS
From the Morning Prayer. Translated by Jacob Sloan.

42 A HYMN ON CREATION
A poem describing "the wonders of creation stemming from God's maj-
esty, His beauty, His stature, His crown, and His garment," from *Hekhalot
Rabbati* ("Greater Hekhalot"), 24:3, which G. G. Scholem dates not later
than the third century. Text and translation: Gershom G. Scholem,
Jewish Gnosticism, Merkabah Mysticism, and Talmudic Judaism, The Jewish
Theological Seminary, New York, 1960, pp. 61 f. Reprinted by per-
mission.

44 MAY THE NAME SEND HIS HIDDEN LIGHT
From the prayer composed by the Kabbalist Jacob ben Jacob ha-Kohen
of Segovia, Castile, about 1265. The text, based on a manuscript in the
library of the Jewish Theological Seminary, New York, has been published by G. Scholem in *Maddae ha-Yahadut*, II, Jerusalem, 1927, pp.
220-226. Translated by Jacob Sloan.

46 WHO AT HIS WORD MAKES EVENING FALL
From the Sephardic version of the Evening Service. Translated by Jacob
Sloan.

48 CREATOR OF LIGHT
Call to worship at the Morning Service in the version used during the Days
of Awe. The last paragraph follows the version in the Order of Prayers of
Rav Amram Gaon (Babylonia, 9th cent.), as quoted by S. Baer in his
Seder Avodat Yisrael, Berlin, 1937, p. 76. In worship, the first line is recited
by the Reader, lines 2-8 by the congregation; while the Reader chants "Bless
ye" the congregation prays lines 9-13.

50 SHAPER OF ORIGINS
From *Shaare Zion* ("Gates of Zion"), Prague, 1662, a book of personal

mystical prayers based on the teachings of the great Kabbalists, Isaac Luria and Hayyim Vital Calabrese. The present prayer is from the section for recitation on Sunday. Translated by Jacob Sloan.

52 MEDITATION BEFORE THE "SANCTIFICATION"
A woman's private devotion before the Sanctification (*Kedushah*) is recited in public worship. *Tehinnah,* Sulzbach, 1798. Translated by Jacob Sloan.

54 MEDITATION ON THE CREATION OF MAN
A woman's private prayer for Friday, the day of the creation of man. *Tehinnah,* Sulzbach, 1798, No. 44. Translation: Solomon B. Freehof, "Devotional Literature in the Vernacular," *Central Conference of American Rabbis Yearbook XXXIII,* 1923, pp. 397 f. The prayer continues on the theme of sin and atonement.

56 BLESSING OF THE NEW MOON
The text is talmudic (Sanhedrin 42a). The appearance of the new moon determines the beginning of the Jewish month. The renewal of the moon is taken as a symbol of the revival of Israel; "those borne from the belly" refers to Israel (*see* Isa. 46:3). Translated by Jacob Sloan.

58 A PERFECT WORLD
This benediction is intended to be recited by one "who goes outdoors during the month of Nisan (March-April), and sees trees budding" (Talmud, Berakhot 43b). Translated by Olga Marx.

62 MY SOUL THIRSTETH FOR THEE
Psalm 63:2-5, 8-9. With some occasional changes, the translation of this and the following biblical passages is from *The Holy Scriptures,* published by The Jewish Publication Society of America, Philadelphia.

64 FROM ETERNITY TO ETERNITY
From a prayer entitled *Magen u-Mehayyeh* ("Shield and Quickener") by Saadia Gaon (9th-10th cent.), religious philosopher. Text (from a manuscript in the library of Dropsie College) in B. Halper, *Post-Biblical Hebrew Literature,* Philadelphia, 1921. "To keep them alive": there is a break in the manuscript at this point; the following is not a direct continuation. Translated by Hillel Halkin.

66 WHOSOEVER KNOWETH THY NAME
By Saadia Gaon. Text: *Siddur Rav Saadia Gaon,* ed. I. Davidson, S. Assaf, B. I. Joel, Jerusalem, 1941, p. 379. Translation in *Rab Saadia Gaon: Studies in His Honor,* ed. Louis Finkelstein, New York, 1944, Appendix IV.

68 WITH ALL MY STRENGTH
A poem by Judah Halevi (11th-12th cent.), Spanish Hebrew poet, the greatest in post-biblical Judaism, and religious philosopher. Translated by Olga Marx.

70 LORD, WHERE SHALL I FIND THEE?
From a poem by Judah Halevi. Translation: Nina Salaman, *Selected Poems of Jehudah Halevi,* The Jewish Publication Society, Philadelphia, 1928, pp. 134 f.

72 LORD OF THE UNIVERSE . . . IF YOU HAD CATTLE

The prayer of a shepherd who "did not know how to pray." *Sefer Hasidim* ("Book of the Devout," Germany, 12th-13th cent.), 5-6. A learned man tried to teach the shepherd "the usual prayers, but Heaven interfered. The Merciful One desires the heart only." Translated by Olga Marx.

74 HEART'S COMPANION

By Eleazar Ascari (16th cent., Safed, Palestine), founder of a society dedi-cated to religious devotion. This hymn is still sung in hasidic congregations. Translated by Jacob Sloan.

76 WHOM HAVE I IN HEAVEN BUT THEE?

From *Likkute Tefillot,* a collection of personal prayers ascribed to Nahman of Bratzlav in the Ukraine, 1772-1811, a hasidic master and great-grand-son of Israel Baal Shem Tov, the founder of Hasidism. The present prayer starts with Ps. 73:25-26 and ends with Ps. 86:11 and 51:12. Translated by Jacob Sloan.

80 THE SONG OF "YOU"

Attributed to the hasidic Rabbi Levi Yitzhak of Berditchev (1740-1809), disciple of the Maggid of Mezrich. M. Buber, *Or Haganuz,* Schocken, Jerusalem, 1957, p. 203; the Yiddish source, *ibid.,* p. 478. "Where can I find you," cf. "Lord, Where Shall I Find Thee," in the present section. Translated by Olga Marx and Jacob Sloan.

82 AND YET I PRAY

From *Moderne Psalmen* written by the contemporary composer Arnold Schoenberg; the first part of "Psalm One" was set to music. Translation of the first part: Dika Newlin, *Reconstructionist* XXIV, 19 (1959), p. 21.

86 I TRUST IN THEE

Psalm 31:15-17.

88 MAN'S WAY IS NOT HIS OWN

Jer. 10:23-24.

90 WHAT IS MAN?

Job 7:16b-21. Line 2: Compare Ps. 8:5.

92 O LORD, THOU LOVER OF SOULS

From the apocryphal *Wisdom of Solomon* (11:23-12:1), written by an Alexandrian Jew, probably in the 2nd century B.C.E. The translation is based on R. H. Charles' *Apocrypha and Pseudepigrapha* and the Authorized Version. The re-translation into Hebrew of this and other selections from the Apocrypha is taken from *Ha-Sefarim ha-Hitzonim,* ed. A. Kahana, Tel Aviv, 1936. By permission of The Clarendon Press, Oxford.

94 I WAS RESOLVED TO DO HIS WILL

A free translation of a sonnet by Judah Leon Moscato (Italy, 16th cent.). Text from J. Schirmann, *Mivhar ha-Shirah ha-Ivrit be-Italia,* Schocken, Berlin, 1934. Translated by Olga Marx.

96 GOD, GOD OF THE SPIRITS

From the liturgical work *Shaar ha-Shamayim* ("Gate of Heaven") of Isaiah Halevi Horovitz (born ca. 1555 in Prague, died ca. 1625 in Safed, Palestine), author of *Shene Luhot ha-Berit* ("The Two Tables of the Covenant"). "At all times . . .": Eccles. 9:8. "To behold . . .": Ps. 27:4; 29:9. Translated by Jacob Sloan.

98 THOU AND I

From a handwritten prayer book of the Yemenite Jews. Translation: Herbert Weiner, in *The Bridge: A Yearbook of Judaeo-Christian Studies,* III, New York, 1958, pp. 25f.

100 ENABLE US TO BREAK DESIRE

From *Likkute Tefillot,* ascribed to Nahman of Bratzlav. Lublin, 1914, I, p. 259.

102 HUMILITY

From *Likkute Tefillot,* II, p. 117. "I shall not die": Ps. 118:17.

104 FATHER OF ALL WORLDLY THINGS

From a poem by Hillel Zeitlin (1872-1943), representative of hasidic thought in modern Yiddish literature. Zeitlin was killed in the Warsaw ghetto. Translation: Hillel Halkin.

106 FORGIVE ME

A poem, originally entitled "Prayer," by Abraham Shlonsky (b. 1900), Israeli poet. Translated by Arnold Band.

110 FROM THE DEPTHS I CALLED THEE

Psalm 130 (*De profundis*), recited as part of the Morning Prayer during the Days of Awe. Translated by Jacob Sloan.

112 THE LORD IS MY SHEPHERD

Psalm 23. It is sung during the Third Meal on Sabbath afternoon.

114 I SAT ALONE BECAUSE OF THY HAND

Jer. 15:15-18.

116 IN MY STRAITS I CALLED

Jonah's prayer "from out of the fish's belly" (Jonah 2:3-10). The book of Jonah is read during the Afternoon Service on the Day of Atonement. Translated by Jacob Sloan.

120 THOU HAST HELPED ME TO SALVATION

From the apocryphal *Psalms of Solomon* (16:5-6, 9-10, 12), written in Hebrew in the middle of the first cent. B.C.E. and preserved in Greek translation. The translation follows R. H. Charles' *Apocrypha and Pseudepigrapha.*

122 THE WORLD LIES IN DARKNESS

From the apocryphal *Fourth Book of Ezra* (14:18, 20-22), an apocalypse, written in Hebrew or Aramaic after the destruction of the Second Temple. The present passage is Ezra's prayer for inspiration to restore the sacred Scriptures. The translation from versions based on a lost Greek rendition of the original follows G. H. Box, in R. H. Charles, *Apocrypha and Pseudepigrapha.*

124 HEAR OUR VOICE

From the Penitential Service (*Selihot*) held before dawn on and before the Days of Awe. Beginning with the fifth line, this prayer is composed of biblical quotations: Lam. 5:21; Ps. 5:2; 19:15; 51:13; 71:9; 38:22; 86:7. The "I" and "My" of the Psalmist were transformed into a communal "We" and "Our," a change which was criticized by some medieval theologians. Translated by Jacob Sloan.

126 THE GATES OF MERCY

From the *Apostolic Constitutions*, a collection of ecclesiastical material of Syrian origin (late 4th cent. but based on older sources). Its seventh and eighth books contain fragments of Jewish liturgy with minor interpolations by which Christians had adapted the prayers for their own use. W. Bousset, "Eine jüdische Gebetsammlung etc." *Nachrichten von der K. Gesellschaft der Wissenschaften in Göttingen,* Philologische-Historische Klasse 1915, pp. 435-485, and Erwin R. Goodenough, *By Light, Light. The Mystic Gospel of Hellenistic Judaism,* New Haven, 1935, ch. XI. The present text is Fragment V (Apost. Const. VII, 33:2-7); the interpolations have been omitted. Goodenough, *op. cit.,* pp. 316f. "I will make . . .": Gen. 22:17.

128 THE GOD OF THEM THAT REPENT

From the apocryphal "Prayer of Manasseh, King of Judah when he was holden captive in Babylon" (see II Chron. 33:11-13, 18-19), preserved in the 3rd cent. Christian work, *Didaskalia.* The translation follows the Authorized Version.

130 LET ME RETURN

From a poem attributed to Bahya ibn Pakuda (Spain, 11th cent.), ethical philosopher, author of *Hovot ha-Levavot* ("The Duties of the Heart"). "Create for me . . .": Ps. 51:12. Translation: *Sabbath Prayer Book,* Jewish Reconstructionist Foundation, New York. Reprinted by permission.

132 GIVE ME A GOOD HEART

A private prayer from the liturgy of the Karaites, the Bible-centered, anti-rabbinic sect, founded in the eighth cent. Text: *Seder ha-Tefillot ke-Minhag ha-Karaim,* I, Vilna, 1891, p. 157. Translation: Leon Nemoy, *Karaite Anthology,* Yale University Press, New Haven, 1952, pp. 320f. Reprinted by permission.

134 DO YOUR WILL

One of the "short prayers" mentioned by the Talmud (Berakhot 29b), to be recited by a person in danger. Translated by Jacob Sloan.

138 THE SOUL YOU HAVE PLACED IN ME

A meditation upon arising (Talmud, Berakhot 60b). It was incorporated in the Morning Prayer. Translated by Jacob Sloan.

140 GRACE AFTER MEALS

The first stanza. Translated by Olga Marx.

142 CREATOR OF MANY SOULS

Benediction recited after partaking of certain foods. (See Talmud, Berakhot 37a and 44a.) Translated by Jacob Sloan.

144 AFTER DELIVERANCE FROM DANGER

A benediction recited during the Torah Reading Service by persons who have been in peril of their lives upon their deliverance or recovery. The

Response is recited by the congregation. Source: Talmud, Berakhot 54b, and Maimonides, *Mishneh Torah,* Hilkhot Berakhot X, 8.

146 MY FATHER ART THOU

The Book of Sirach 51:1-2, 6-11. Translation follows the Charles edition of the Apocrypha and Pseudepigrapha.

148 WISE IN THY TRUTH

Thanksgiving Psalms (Hodayot) of the Qumran (Dead Sea) Community, VII, 26-31. Text: A. M. Habermann, *Megillot Midbar Yehudah,* Jerusalem, 1959, p. 123. Translation: Theodor H. Gaster, *The Dead Sea Scriptures.* Doubleday Anchor Books, Garden City, N. Y., 1956, p. 163. Reprinted by permission.

150 STREAMS IN DRY GROUND

Thanksgiving Psalms (Hodayot), VIII, 4-8. Text: A. M. Habermann, *op. cit.,* p. 123. Translation: Millar Burrows, *The Dead Sea Scrolls,* New York, 1955, p. 411. Copyright © 1955 by Millar Burrows. Reprinted by permission of The Viking Press, Inc.

152 WELL I KNOW

From a long prayer by Saadia Gaon. *Siddur Rav Saadia Gaon,* edited by I. Davidson, Jerusalem, 1941, pp. 64f. "Life and mercy . . .": Job 10:12. Translated by Jacob Sloan.

154 FATHER OF LIFE

A hymn to life by Joseph Hayyim Brenner (1881-1921), Hebrew author, basically a pessimist and heretic. The translation follows Shalom Spiegel, *Hebrew Reborn,* Meridian Books and The Jewish Publication Society of America, New York, 1962, p. 384.

156 BLESSING OF DEATH

By Nachman Syrkin (1868-1924), Zionist and Socialist leader, written shortly before his death. As he grew older, the radical and anti-clerical allowed his deep religious sense to assume ancestral forms.—The river Yabok, tributary of the Jordan, is, in Jewish tradition, a symbol of transition from life to death. Translated by Ben Halpern in Marie Syrkin, *Nachman Syrkin,* New York, 1961, p. 226.

160 WITH THEE IS WISDOM

From the apocryphal *Wisdom of Solomon* (9:1-4, 9-10). The translation follows the Authorized Version.

162 THE GIFT OF KNOWLEDGE

One of the Eighteen Benedictions, the main weekday prayer. Translated by Jacob Sloan.

164 OUR FATHER, THE FATHER COMPASSIONATE

From the Morning Prayer. This passage is followed by the proclamation of the unity of God ("Hear, O Israel"). Translated by Jacob Sloan.

166 THOU HAST TAUGHT US KNOWLEDGE

A hymn at the conclusion of the Qumran (Dead Sea) Community's *Manual of Discipline.* Text: A. M. Habermann, *Megillot Midbar Yehudah,* Jerusalem, 1959, p. 70. Translation: Theodor H. Gaster, *The Dead Sea*

Scriptures, Doubleday Anchor Books, Garden City, N. Y., 1956, pp. 121f. Reprinted by permission.

168 THAT THY TORAH BE OUR CRAFT

A private prayer of Rabbi Hiyya; Talmud, Berakhot 16b. Translated by Olga Marx.

170 THE CROWN OF TORAH

A prayer attributed to King David. *Seder Eliyahu Rabba* XVIII.

174 THE BLESSING AFTER THE CIRCUMCISION

The concluding section of the Service at a Circumcision. The biblical quotations: Prov. 23:25, Ezek. 16:6, Ps. 118:1.

176 BRIDEGROOM AND BRIDE

The concluding section of the Marriage Service, after which a glass is broken by the bridegroom, in remembrance of the destruction of Zion.

178 GRANT THEM MERCY

Prayer of Raguel after the marriage of his daughter Sarah to Tobias, son of the pious Tobit. Sarah's previous husbands were successively killed by the demon Asmodeus upon the wedding night of each; Tobias succeeded in driving away the demon. From the apocryphal *Book of Tobit* (8:15-17), written, probably in Aramaic, in the pre-Maccabean period, and preserved mainly in Greek recensions; recently fragments of the book were found among the writings of the Qumran (Dead Sea) Community. The translation follows the Authorized Version.

180 INTO THINE HAND

From the Evening Prayer. "In whose hand . . .": Job 12:10. "Into thine hand . . .": Ps. 31:6.

182 WHO DROPS THE BONDS OF SLEEP

Prayer before going to sleep. Translated by Jacob Sloan.

184 BLESS THOU . . . THIS YEAR

One of the Eighteen Benedictions, the main weekday prayer. Translated by Jacob Sloan.

186 THOU GIVEST ALL, TAKING NOUGHT

A papyrus leaf from a liturgic book, written in Greek, and found in Egypt. Joseph Warhaftig ("A Jewish Prayer in a Greek Papyrus," *Journal of Theological Studies,* Oxford, XL, 1939, pp. 376-381) and A. Marmorstein ("The Oldest Form of the Eighteen Benedictions," *Jewish Quarterly Review* XXXIV, 1943, pp. 137-159) recognized in this text a translation of the "oldest form of Jewish prayer used in the last century of the Temple." Text and translation: H. I. Bell and T. C. Skeat, *Fragments of an Unknown Gospel and Other Early Christian Papyri,* London, 1935, pp. 58f.

190 WHO FORMED YOU IN JUDGMENT

A benediction to be recited on entering a cemetery. Original versions of this prayer are to be found in the Talmud, Berakhot 58b. "Who formed you" i.e., the dead buried here. Translated by Olga Marx.

192 KADDISH

Originally a prayer for the coming of the kingdom of God, recited at the conclusion of a public study session, the Kaddish developed into a part of the synagogal liturgy (first mention as such in the Palestinian Tractate *Soferim*, ca. 600 C.E.). The custom of reciting the Kaddish during the year of mourning for parents originated in medieval Germany. The central theme, "Let His great name be blessed . . ." alludes to Dan. 2:20 and is mentioned in Sifre Deut., No. 306, and in the Talmud, Berakhot 3a. Comp. also the first paragraph with Matt. 6:9-10.

194 MEMORIAL PRAYER
From the Burial and Memorial Service. The translation is based on a rendition by Judah Goldin (*Jewish Frontier*, November, 1954).

198 WATCHMAN OF ISRAEL
From the Morning Prayer. According to some rites, it is a prayer for Fast and Penitential days. Translated by Jacob Sloan.

200 OUR EYES ARE LONGING
Written by Yannai, who lived in Palestine, ca. 600. The poem has as its inspiration Gen. 29:31-32: "The Lord saw that Leah was hated . . . She said, 'He has looked upon my affliction.' " Text, edited by Menahem Zulay, in *Almanach des Schocken Verlags 5699*, Berlin, 1938-39, p. 6. Translated by Olga Marx.

202 OUR BROTHERS, ALL THE HOUSE OF ISRAEL
Recited on Mondays and Thursdays before the Torah is returned to the Ark. It goes back to the Order of Prayers of Rav Amram Gaon (Babylonia, 9th cent.). Translated by Jacob Sloan.

204 THOU HAST MADE ME HUNGER
Bahya ibn Pakuda (*Hovot ha-Levavot* X, 1) mentions a saint who used to arise in the middle of the night to recite this prayer. "Though He cut me down": Job 13:15. Translated by Jacob Sloan.

206 AGAINST THE WILL OF HEAVEN
Words of an exile from Spain, 1492, after having been "put ashore at some uninhabited place" and having witnessed the death of his wife and two children. *Shevet Yehudah*, by Solomon ibn Verga (Spain-Italy, 15th-16th cent.) ch. LII.

208 THE MARTYR'S PRAYER
From *Shene Luhot ha-Berit* ("The Two Tables of the Covenant") by Isaiah Halevi Horovitz of Prague and Safed (*ca. 1555-ca. 1625*). "Ten Martyrs"— in the period of persecution under Hadrian after the end of the revolt of Bar Kokhba (132-135 C.E.). On the prayer, see Jacob Katz, "Martyrdom in the Middle Ages and in 1648-1649" (Hebrew), *Y. F. Baer Jubilee Volume*, Jerusalem, 1960, pp. 325 ff.

210 A MARRANO'S PRAYER UPON AWAKENING
From a collection of prayers preserved by Portuguese Marranos (Jews converted to Christianity under pressure who, however, secretly adhered to their ancestral faith). Samuel Schwarz, *Os Christàos Novos em Portugal no seculo xx*, Lisbon, 1925. Translated by Denah Lida.

212 A MARRANO'S MORNING PRAYER
See preceding note.

214 A BAR MITZVAH PRAYER

Words spoken by a boy named Shmuel at an improvised Bar Mitzvah ceremony at a DP camp in liberated Germany as reported by Gottfried Neuburger in "An Orthodox G. I. Fights a War," *Commentary* VII, 3 (March 1949), p. 271.

216 PASSOVER, BERGEN-BELSEN, 1944

The Jewish prisoners at the German concentration camp at Bergen-Belsen did not have *Matzah* for the observance of Passover in 1944. Under the circumstances the sages at the camp permitted the eating of leavened bread for which occasion this benediction was composed. The text was published in *Yediot Bet Lohamey ha-Getaot*, 14-15 (*Kibbutz Lohamey ha-Getaot*, Haifa). Translation: Philip Goodman, *The Passover Anthology*, The Jewish Publication Society, Philadelphia, 1961, p. 383. "And ye shall live": Lev. 18:5.

218 LORD, I WANT TO RETURN

A poem by Karl Wolfskehl (1869-1948), German-Jewish poet who in his *Die Stimme spricht* (Schocken, 1936; English edition, *1933: A Poem Sequence*, translated by Carol North Valhope and Ernst Morwitz, Schocken Books, New York, 1947) gave voice to the tragedy of the period.

222 ROCK OF ISRAEL

From the Morning Prayer. Translated by Jacob Sloan.

226 WHEN A FOREIGNER

From King Solomon's prayer at the dedication of the Temple in Jerusalem. I Kings 8:41ff.

228 LEAVE US NOT

Jer. 14:7ff.

230 THY CITY AND THY PEOPLE

Daniel 9:18f. From the *Tahanun* prayer, recited on Mondays and Thursdays.

232 JERUSALEM, THOU HOLY CITY

The Book of Tobit 13:1-4, 7, 9, 14ff. (Authorized Version).

234 TAKE PITY, O LORD

A passage from the Grace after Meals. The text follows the Sephardic version. Translated by Jacob Sloan.

236 COMFORT, O LORD

Prayer for the Afternoon Service on the feast of the Ninth of Av, which commemorates the destruction of Jerusalem. The original form of the prayer appears in Yer. Berakhot IV (8a). "As for me . . .": Zech. 2:9.

240 FROM A JUDAEO-GREEK LAMENT

From a Greek poem in Hebrew characters inscribed on the end papers of a manuscript Mahzor in the Library of the Jewish Theological Seminary (Adler ms. 726), written probably before the middle of the 15th century. Its theme is the exile after the first fall of Jerusalem. The dialect is northern vulgate, a Greek "Yiddish." Edited and translated by Benjamin Schwartz in *The Joshua Bloch Memorial Volume*, New York Public Library, New York, 1960. Each line is preceded by *ochou* (alas) and ended by *aa* (ah!).

242 THE SANCTITY OF ZION

A woman's private prayer. *Tehinnot u-Vakashot,* Jerusalem, 1862, pp. 23f. Translated by Jacob Sloan.

244 O GOD, SAVE MASADA

From the poem *Masada,* by Yitzhak Lamdan (1899-1954), Tel Aviv, 1927, pp. 65ff., abridged. Masada was the last fortress of Judaea to be conquered by the Romans in 73 C.E. Translation: Simon Halkin, *Modern Hebrew Literature,* Schocken Books, New York, 1950, p. 129.

246 BEFORE THE BATTLE

A poem, originally entitled "Prayer," by Hayyim Guri (b. 1923), Israeli poet. *Pirhe Esh,* Jerusalem, 1961, p. 58. Translated by Arnold Band.

248 THE RETURN

From the *Amidah* (Prayer of Benedictions).

252 ACCEPT OUR REST

From the *Amidah* (Prayer of Benedictions) in the Friday Evening Service.

254 BLESSED BE THE NAME

From the *Zohar* ("Book of Splendor") II, 369; the introductory passage reads: "When the Torah scroll is taken out to be read in public, the gates of compassion open in heaven and awaken the supernal love." This hymm (written in Aramaic), which under the influence of Kabbalah became a part of the liturgy after 1600, is read on Sabbaths in the Service for taking out the Torah.

258 LORD OF ALL EONS

A free translation of a Sabbath hymm written in Aramaic by Israel Najara, mystical poet, born at Safed about the middle of the 16th cent. Translated by Olga Marx.

260 A MEDITATION BEFORE THE CONCLUSION OF THE SABBATH

A prayer for women. *Shas Tehinnah Hadashah,* Vilna, 1931, p. 154.

262 WHO SETS APART THE SACRED AND PROFANE

A free rendition of a hymm attributed to Isaac ibn Ghayyat (Spain, 11th cent.). It is sung at the close of the Sabbath after the *Havdalah,* the bene- diction of separation (between the Holy and the Profane), and recited over wine, spices, and light. Translated by Olga Marx.

264 GOD OF ABRAHAM

A prayer recited by Jewish mothers at the close of the Sabbath. Prilutzki, *Jüdische Volkslieder,* Warsaw, 1911 and 1913, and Arno Nadel, "Jüdische Volkslieder," *Der Jude* I, 1916-1917, p. 192. Translated by Olga Marx.

270 GRANT THY AWE

From the Prayer of Benedictions for the Days of Awe. "The Lord will reign": Ps. 146:10. Translated by Olga Marx.

272 IT IS FOR US TO PRAISE

Ascribed to Rav, talmudic master of the 3rd century and head of the academy of Sura, Babylonia. The hymn is a part of the Additional Service of the New Year's Day. Since 1300, it has served as the conclusion of the daily prayer. Translated by Allen Mandelbaum.

274 THEREFORE WE HOPE FOR THEE

Continuation of the preceding passage. In the New Year's Day liturgy it serves as an introduction to *Malkhuyot,* the affirmation of the divine kingship. Translated by Allen Mandelbaum.

276 REIGN OVER ALL THE UNIVERSE

The concluding section of the *Malkhuyot*-liturgy. Translated by Jacob Sloan.

278 REMEMBRANCE

In the Additional Service for the New Year's Day, the theme of "Kingship" is followed by the theme of "Remembrance" (*Zikhronot*) of human deeds and of divine judgment. A third theme—Redemption—concludes the trilogy. Translated by Jacob Sloan.

280 BEFORE I WAS FORMED

A confession composed by talmudic masters (Yoma 87b), later incorporated in the service for the Day of Atonement. Translated by Jacob Sloan.

282 OUR GOD WHO ART IN HEAVEN

From the Penitential Service (*Selihot*) in the Sephardic liturgy for the Days of Awe. *The Form of Prayers . . . of the Spanish and Portuguese Jews: New-Year Service,* ed. by Isaac Leeser, Philadelphia, 5613 (1853), pp. 17ff. The line, "give life and peace to our sovereign lord the king" carries the note: "In a republic: to the officers of government."

284 I SHALL FLEE FROM THEE TO THEE

From *Keter Malkhut* ("The Kingly Crown") by Solomon ibn Gabirol (see above), ch. XXXVIII and XL (selected). "Though Thou kill me": cf. Job 13:15. "I will not . . .": Gen. 32:26. "I praise Thee": cf. Isa. 12:1. Translation: Bernard Lewis, *The Kingly Crown,* Vallentine, Mitchell, London, 1961, pp. 62f. and 67. In the traditional liturgy, the *Keter Malkhut* is read after the conclusion of the *Kol Nidre* Service. By permission of Vallentine, Mitchell & Co., Ltd.

286 THE READER'S PRAYER

A medieval prayer recited by the cantor at the beginning of the services at the Days of Awe. "Let our banner be love": cf. Cant. 2:4. "Truth and peace . . .": Zech. 8:19.

290 THOU GIVEST A HAND TO TRANSGRESSORS

From the *Neilah* (Closing) Service for the Day of Atonement. "Seek the Lord": Isa. 55:6.

292 THE DWELLERS ON HIGH

"Before reciting the Prayer of Benedictions on New Year's Day, Rabbi Levi Yitzhak of Berditchev sang. . . ." Translated by Allen Mandelbaum. *Eser Orot* ("Ten Lights", collection of Hasidica), Warsaw, 1913, and M. Buber, *Or ha-Ganuz,* Schocken, Jerusalem, 1957, p. 201. The translation is based on the rendition by Olga Marx in M. Buber, *Tales of the Hasidim: The Early Masters,* Schocken Books, New York, 1947, p. 209.

294 ILLUMINE MY EYES

A prayer by Abraham Isaac Kook (1865-1935), Ashkenazic Chief Rabbi of Palestine (1921-1935), author of *Orot ha-Kodesh* ("The Light of Holiness") and a *Commentary to the Prayer Book*. The translation follows Ben Zion Bokser, *The High Holyday Prayer Book,* New York, 1959. p. 255. By permission of the Hebrew Publishing Company.

296 OPEN UNTO US THE GATE

From the *Neilah* (Closing) Service for the Day of Atonement.

298 THE CLOSING OF THE GATE

From a poem attributed to Moses ibn Ezra (Spain, 11th-12th cent.), chanted, in the Sephardic rite, as a prelude to the *Neilah* (Closing) Service for the Day of Atonement. Translated by Allen Mandelbaum.

302 SET PEACE, GOODNESS AND BLESSING

From the Morning Prayer. Translated by Jacob Sloan.

304 WALK ME IN PEACE

A prayer before starting out on a journey; Talmud, Berakhot 29b. Translated by Jacob Sloan.

306 LOVE AND BROTHERLINESS

A meditation of the talmudic master Eleazar (third cent.); Berakhot 16b. Translated by Olga Marx.

308 KEEP MY TONGUE FROM EVIL

From the private meditation of the talmudic master Mar bar Ravina (Berakhot 17a). It was later incorporated in the public service. "Be the words . . .": Ps. 19:15. Translated by Olga Marx.

310 NO HATRED

A private prayer of a talmudic master; Yer. Berakhot 7d. Translated by Hillel Halkin.

312 LORD OF PEACE

Ascribed to Nahman of Bratzlav. *Likkute Tefillot* I, 95.

314 ANNUL WARS AND THE SHEDDING OF BLOOD

Ascribed to Nahman of Bratzlav. "Nor again . . .": Isa. 2:4. "To announce . . .": Ps. 145:12. Translated by Jacob Sloan.

316 GUARD US FROM VICIOUS LEANINGS

From the private supplication of the hasidic master Elimelekh of Lizhensk (Poland, 18th cent.), known for his humility. *Dor Deah,* by Y. A. Kamelhar, Bilguray, 1933, p. 127. Translated by Jacob Sloan.

318 MAY HE BLESS THEE

The priestly blessing of the Qumran (Dead Sea) Community; it is an expansion of the Aaronide blessing, Num. 6:22-26. *Manual of Discipline*, Plate II, lines 2-4. A. M. Habermann, *Megillot Midbar Yehudah,* Jerusalem, 1959, p. 61.

GUIDE TO THE PRAYERS:

Motifs, Occasions, and Uses

Abraham, Isaac, Jacob, 128, 264, 286

Apocryphal, 92, 120, 122, 126, 128, 146, 160, 178, 186, 232

Biblical, 62, 86, 88, 90, 110, 112, 114, 116′18, 124, 226, 228, 230

Bridegroom and Bride, 176

Burial Service, 190, 194

Cain and Abel, 106

Children, 174, 178, 264′66

Circumcision, 174

Creation, 40′58, 104, 140, 142, 270, 278

Creation of Man, 54, 152, 160

Days of Awe, 270′98

Death, 90, 112, 120, 146, 156, 180, 182, 190, 192, 194, 284

Deliverance, 146, 182, 228, 258, 262, 294, 298

Destruction of the Temple, 236′38

Elijah, 264′66

Evening Prayer, 46, 162, 180, 182, 184, 248

Exile, 202, 236, 240, 258

Forgiveness, 110, 128, 262, 298

Gentile, 226, 232, 270, 272, 274, 292

God's Love, 44, 74, 92, 200, 286, 292, 294

Grace after Meals, 140, 142, 234

Hasidic, 76, 80, 100, 102, 312, 314, 316

Heart, 50, 68, 76, 130, 164

Holiness, 40, 76, 98, 100, 122, 124, 160, 222, 242, 260, 314

Hope, 110

Humility, 100, 102, 132, 280, 308

Israel, 64, 76, 110, 170, 192, 198, 202, 208, 222, 226, 232, 234, 254-56, 276, 286, 292, 302

Jerusalem, 132, 176, 226, 230, 232, 234, 236, 242, 270

Judgment, 88, 90, 114, 148, 190, 292

Karaite, 132

Kingdom of God, 64, 192, 254-56, 270, 274, 276, 282

Knowledge, 160-70, 318

Land of Israel, 236, 240, 242, 244, 246, 294

Life, 92, 104, 154

Light, 50, 52, 64, 182, 202, 302

Light and Darkness, 44, 48, 122

Loneliness, 114

Love for God, 50, 62, 68, 72, 164, 200, 204, 232

Man in Trouble, 110, 112, 114, 116-18, 130, 132, 144, 146

Marranos, 210, 212

Marriage Service, 176

Martyrdom, 208

Masada, 244

Medieval, 64, 66, 68, 70, 72, 94, 96, 130, 152, 200, 204, 206,
    208, 240, 262, 284, 298

Mercy, 52, 62, 64, 74, 86, 92, 98, 104, 110, 112, 120, 124,
    132, 140, 146, 148, 152, 160, 170, 178, 230, 284, 290,
    294, 304

Modern, 82, 104, 106, 154, 156, 218, 244, 246, 294

Morning Prayer, 40, 48, 138, 162, 164, 184, 198, 202, 222,
    230, 248, 302

Mystical, 42, 44, 50, 74, 254

Naming a Son, 174

Nature, 46, 56, 58, 112, 150, 184

Nazi Period, 214, 216, 218

Nearness of God, 70

Old Age, 124

Passover, 216

Peace, 48, 74, 176, 182, 192, 232, 282, 286-88, 302, 304, 306,
    310, 312, 314, 318

Presence of God, 62-82, 86, 98, 112, 114, 130

Qumran (Dead Sea) Community, 148, 150, 166, 318

Redemption, 180, 202, 216, 222, 260, 282, 298

Repentance, 124, 128, 130, 290

Resurrection, 96, 102, 138, 156, 190

Sabbath, 252-64, 294

Sabbath Prayer, 252, 254-56, 258, 262, 264

Sanctification of the Name, 40, 52, 192, 198, 208, 252

Sin, 90, 92, 94, 128, 208, 228, 262, 284, 286, 290

Sleep, 182

Suffering, 198, 200, 202, 204, 206, 216

Talmudic-Midrashic, 56, 58, 134, 138, 142, 144, 168, 170,
   272, 274, 280, 304, 306, 308, 310

Temple, 226, 234, 236-38, 258

Thanksgiving, 120, 138-56

Time, 46, 56, 86, 94, 184

Torah, 50, 94, 122, 132, 164, 168, 170, 174, 252, 254-56, 276,
   294, 302, 308, 310, 312

Union of Mankind, 270, 274, 276, 312, 314

Wisdom, 148, 152, 160

World to Come, 102, 138, 170, 234

Yemenite, 98

Zion, 226-48

The type face used here for the Hebrew prayers was especially designed in Jerusalem by Francisca Baruch and is called Schocken Hebrew. It is based on the
fifteenth-sixteenth-century North Italian fonts of Soncino and Bomberg. The
English text is set in Poliphilus, a type face also derived from a fifteenth-century
North Italian font, that used in *The Dream of Poliphilus,* printed by Aldus.